*To the author of transformation,
the one who makes all things new.*

MY FLIPPING LIFE

THE FURNITURE FLIPPING GUIDE FOR PEOPLE
WHO WANT MORE THAN JUST A HOBBY

MICHELE CORWIN

My Flipping Life
Copyright © 2019 by Retique It, LLC

All rights reserved. No part of this publication may be reproduced, distributed, or transmitted in any form or by any means, including photocopying, recording, or other electronic or mechanical methods, without the prior written permission of the publisher, except in the case of brief quotations embodied in critical reviews and certain other noncommercial uses permitted by copyright law.

Retique It ® liquid wood references a restorative product sold by Renaissance Innovations, LLC, which is a liquid product that contains 11% emulsified wood by weight and is 66% wood by volume. Retique It ®, the content in this book, and any trademarks referenced in this book are not associated with, nor is such content endorsed by, the trademark LIQUIDWOOD® or its owner Abatron, Inc.

Retique It ® is a registered trademark of Renaissance Innovations LLC.

All content contained herein is the property of Retique It, LLC, and may not be used without the express written consent of Retique It, LLC.

Retique It, LLC, does not have any affiliation with, nor has any endorsement of sponsorship been provided by any trademarks referenced herein or the owners of those respective trademarks.

All trademarks contained herein are used for reference and commentary purpose and owned by their registered owners.

First Printing, 2019
ISBN 978-1-7331084-0-9
www.FlipYourLiving.com

Cover Design: Paola Amparan
Interior Layout and Graphics: Paola Amparan
Photography: Paola Amparan
(Unless otherwise credited. Photography on page 19, pages 25 - 28, page 45, page 61, and page 83 by Michele Corwin)

Furniture Illustrations on page 1, pages 8-12, and page 186 by Henry G. McCarthy

CONTENTS

INTRODUCTION - HUMBLE BEGINNINGS 14
    Quick Start 22

GETTING STARTED
    The Snowball Effect 32
    Flip Your Living 42
    Painting Techniques & Supplies 50
    Why Chalk Finish Paint 56
    The Secret of Retique It 66
    Staging, Lighting, & Photography 74

PROJECT TUTORIALS
    Victorian-Inspired Dining Room Set 86
    French Provincial Drum Table 94
    Versatile Console Table 100
    Ornate Vintage Bedroom Set 108
    Setting up Your WorkStation 116

GETTING DOWN TO BUSINESS
    Pitfalls - Roaches, Smoke, & Strange Characters 122
    Selling Sites, & Pricing 134
    Haggling 144
    More Than a Hobby 152
    The Sky Is Not the Limit 160

TROUBLESHOOTING & PAINTING TECHNIQUES 170

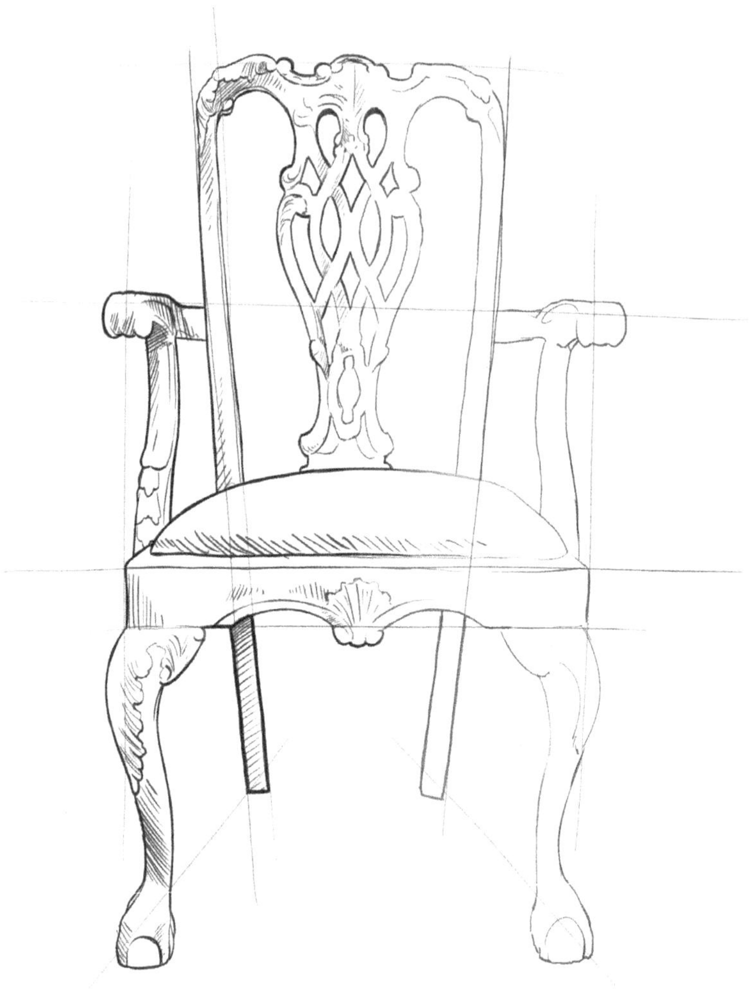

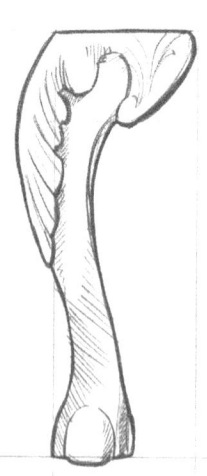

VICTORIAN

ROMANTIC INFLUENCES WITH A GREAT EMPHASIS ON ELABORATE ORNIMENTATION, DARK FINISHES, EMBELISHMENTS AND HEAVY PROPORTIONS. LAVISH AND RICH IN TEXTURE AND MATERIAL.

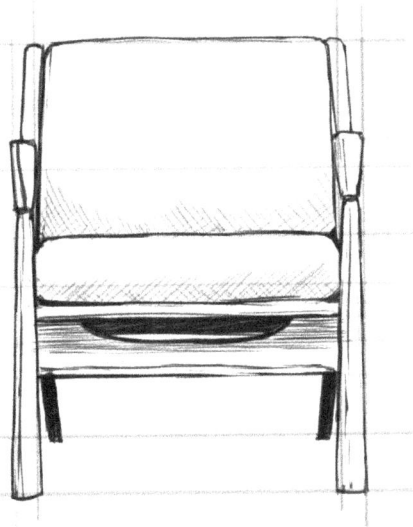

MIDCENTURY MODERN

CHARACTERIZED BY CLEAN LINES, ORGANIC, STREAMLINED FORMS, AND LACK OF EMBELLISHMENT. EXPRESSES HONESTY IN MATERIALITY BY SHOWCASING THE NATURAL TEXTURES OF ITS CONSTRUCTION

FARMHOUSE

RUSTIC CHARM WITH A MIXTURE OF CLASSIC COLORS, WHITES AND WARM WEATHERED WOODS. FOCUSES ON REUSED OR RECYCLED MATERIALS USUALLY GIVING IT A VISUALLY AND PHYSICALLY HEAVIER APPEARANCE AND STATURE.

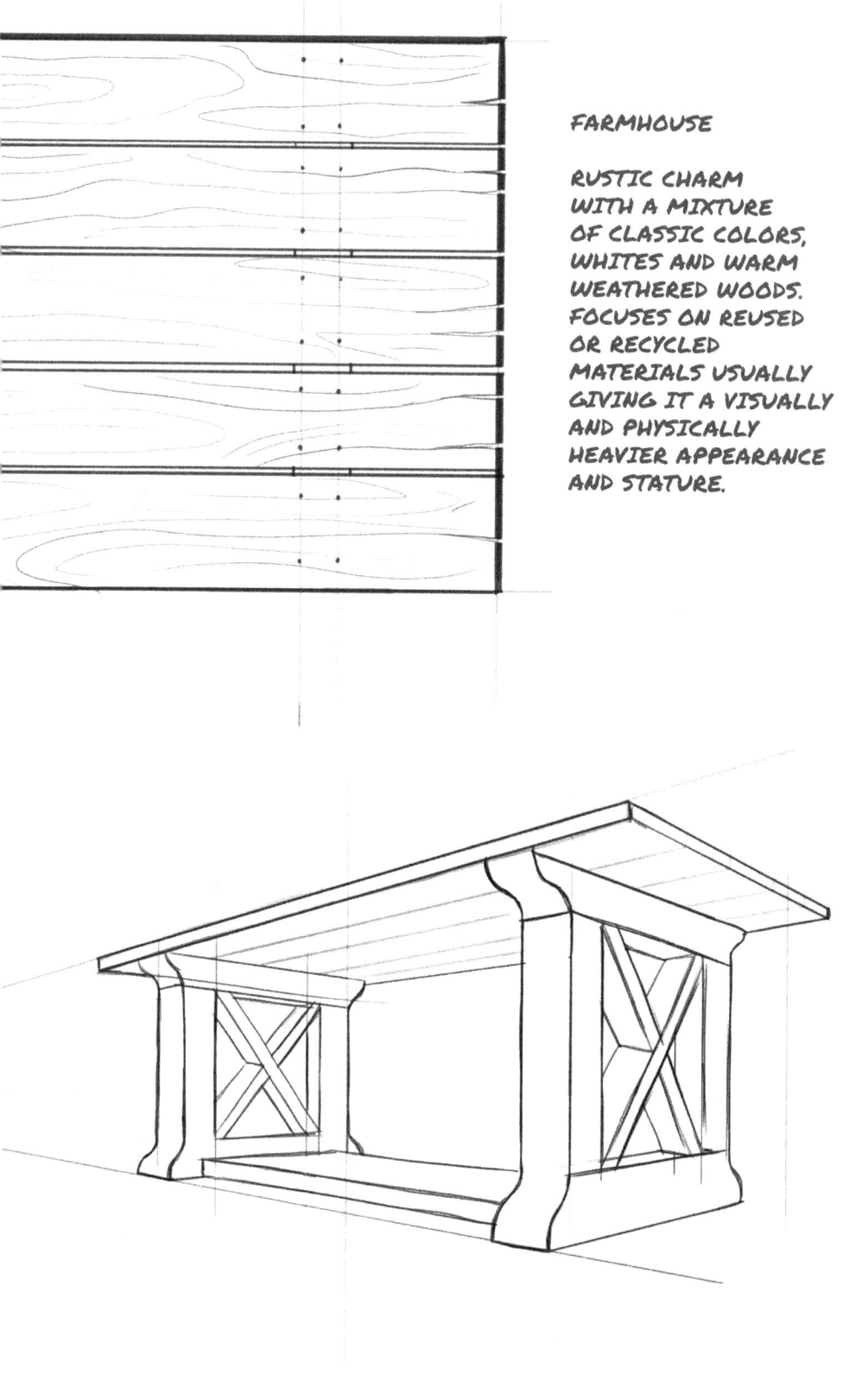

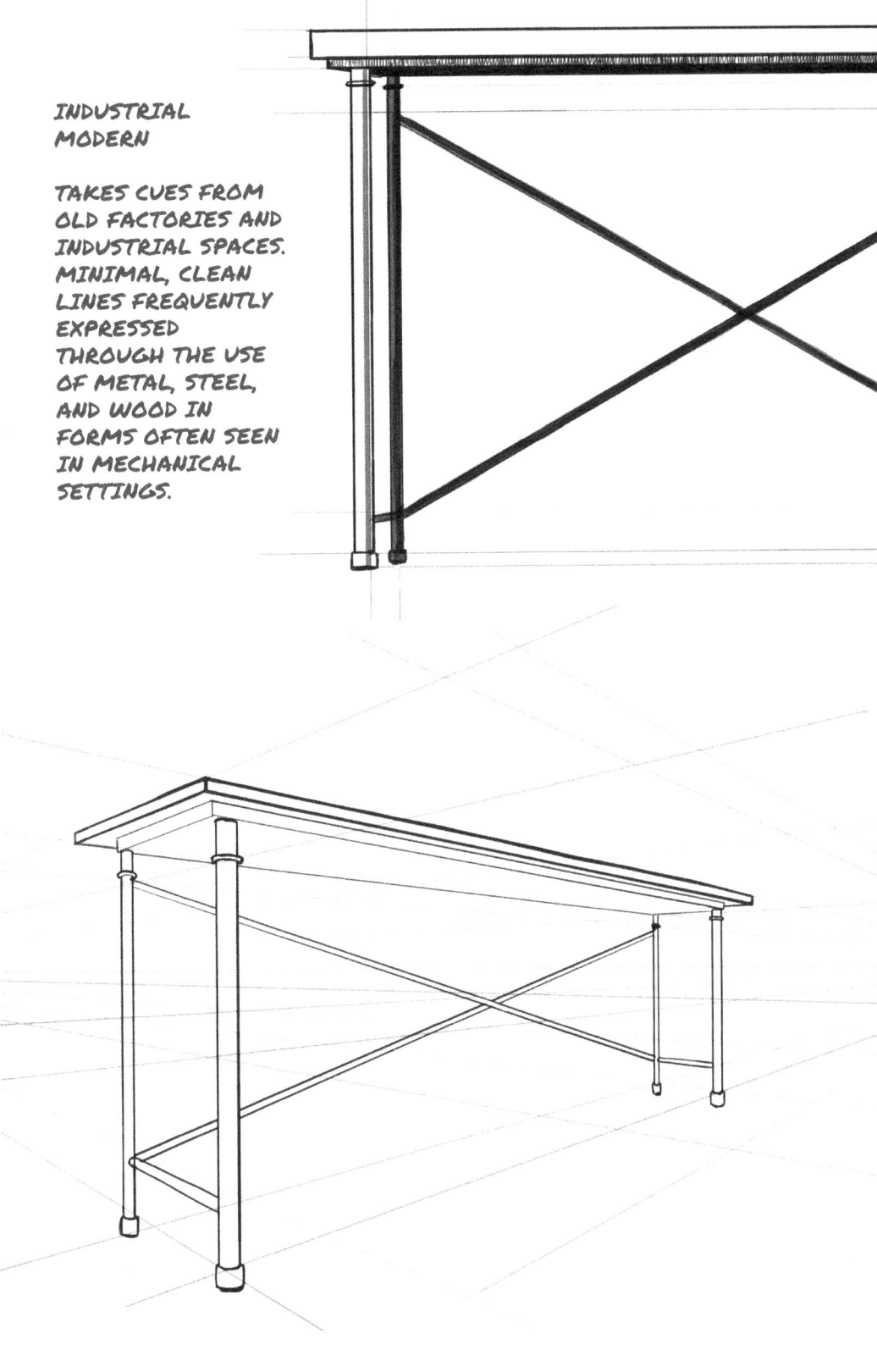

FRENCH PROVINCIAL

FLOWING CURVES WITH DELICATE DETAILS AND OCCASIONAL METALLIC ACCENTS. FREQUENTLY CARVED FROM WOOD. IT IS REMINISCENT OF THE ARTISANS OF THE 18TH CENTURY FRENCH COUNTRYSIDE

Dear reader,

May this book be a beautiful reminder that you will never be a success until you seek out where your joy really comes from. It took me until my mid-thirties to figure this out, and I'm still always learning... ever seeking. My hope for you is that you learn to dig deep and figure out what puts a smile on your face and brings you that spark, that inspiration! You can start small and with something that seems rather silly to others, but is meaningful to you. It can be something completely unique, but it brings you real happiness and tranquility.

For me, that has been redoing furniture and helping others beautify their homes. I don't seek out perfection in my furniture-flips. I'm not a painter who achieves perfection, nor do I get hypercritical of my work during the process. I never judge it until the end, when I can take a step back and look at it—when I can see the bigger picture. Now, it's strange to me how I wasn't living my life this way all along. If we could just all learn to take a step back in our lives and look at ourselves as people who have been dragged through the dirt of life and gotten a little damaged over the years... Thankfully, at any point, we can take a step back, clean ourselves up, and move forward (pull the cobwebs away, so to speak).

It's all fixable—that's what I've learned. Some furniture flips are a lot harder than others. The difficult ones are much more rewarding in the end, though. I can't quite explain why, but they just are. Maybe it's because of the extra time and care invested. But no matter how hard we try, these flips will not be perfect. There will always be a small flaw or a tiny scratch that I know is there but that nobody may ever see unless they take a close look. I have learned to appreciate these small flaws because they can give a piece of furniture character and that oh-so-coveted vintage vibe that people are seeking these days.

I think the transformation process brings about a sort of high for me. For you, your passion may be something else entirely or in a completely different niche. Regardless, I want you to enjoy the transformation you'll read about with my own personal story and similarly through the pictures of furniture you are about to see. And maybe, in some small way, you'll see your life reflected in my journey.

Each of the pieces of furniture shown in this book serves as a sweet little metaphor for the lovely process of change that takes place within each one of us on a much grander scale. In much the same way as "Re-tiqued" furniture, I want you to experience the satisfaction in learning to love yourself—flaws and all—and realize the inner beauty and character that comes from life's struggles. Instead of wishing for perfection, may we always grab hold of the power to recreate ourselves at any moment if we so choose.

Love and blessings,

Michele Corwin

Michele Corwin

INTRODUCTION

HUMBLE BEGINNINGS

> "Sometimes you will never know the value of a moment until it becomes a memory."
>
> Theodor Seuss Geisel - Dr. Seuss

Once it was loved, and once it was new, but as the years flew by, it became covered in dirt and was shut away in darkness for what seemed to be an eternity. This was my ten-dollar table, years ago—the table to which families came together to eat, do homework, and make memories. It was hard to believe it was once new and part of a home, but the faint crayon marks and smears of peanut butter and jelly could still be seen. The smears almost appeared to be baby-finger-sized streaks running toward the edge. There was no denying the table once had simple beauty, but over time, it had become damaged and worn. Years went by, and it was like my life and all the silly dreams I held dear: tucked away, but still there in a forgotten place.

Covered in a burial cloth, my ten-dollar table had been left to sit, while the sticky goo and mess of life became embedded in its soul. It sounds peculiar, but when I think back, that is what the table had come to represent to me. It was a metaphorical mirror of my life, and after seeing the reflection, I was determined to revive it and make it more beautiful than before. This was the humble beginning of my new life and where the story begins.

I was a fighter and desperately wanted a way to help my family make some extra money. I tried selling everything from makeup to diet shakes. We have a large family. I tell people we're like the Brady Bunch if they'd decided to have two more kids. Lots of mouths to feed and lots of butts to wipe. I was busy just trying to take care of the kids, but I knew that, very soon, I'd have to go back to work. This was an unlikely prospect, though, because of the cost of daycare and the fact we had no family to help watch the kids. I was formerly an accountant, with ten years on the job, and I remembered seeing other people succeeding with their thriving businesses. I had dreamed I could have a business of my own that I was passionate about.

You've probably heard the saying about following your heart to find your calling, to do something you love. I always thought this was a pipe dream. Surely, it couldn't be that simple, or everyone would be successful, right? Well, the older I get, the more I see truth in that simple saying, "Follow your bliss." coined by Joseph Campbell. Campbell expounds this idea in the following:

"If you do follow your bliss, you put yourself on a kind of track that has been there all the while, waiting for you, and the life that you ought to be living is the one you are living."

(Please keep this in mind throughout this book.)

So, back to the ten-dollar table. I had really gotten into Pinterest and would drool over the gorgeous pictures of homes and all the furnishings. I'd look at our old hand-me-down dressers and tables, which I was grateful for, but I dreamed of having just one room that looked like it belonged on an HGTV show.

One day—though I'm not exactly sure how, when, or where—I stumbled across an article about people flipping furniture for profit. I thought it would be something I could try because it didn't really require much investment. I watched a couple of YouTube tutorials, and voila! I felt I was a pro and could start painting furniture. I read up and found there was this special paint that had the word "chalk" in it, and it sounded magical. The makers touted how there was no sanding and no real prep work involved. I thought, "I gotta try this!" Sadly, I found out this paint was quite pricey. Nonetheless, I talked my hubby, James, into dragging the kids out of the house to take me to an old antique store that was about a thirty-minute drive from our home. We were going to buy some of the amazing paint everyone was raving about on the internet.

Once we got near the antique store, I started doubting myself. As our old minivan crunched along the unpaved gravel road, I thought to myself, "What am I doing? I can barely paint a wall without messing it up, and now I'm getting ready to waste a Saturday at this old junky antique store that looks like a village of tiny dilapidated houses decorated with wind chimes made from rusty scrap metal?"

As James and I were getting the kids out of the minivan and bringing out the baby carrier, I detected a slight grin on my James' face. Later, I learned he was getting a chuckle out of this, but he wanted to be supportive, even though, to him, he was supporting something he thought would be solely for my entertainment rather than the first step of a highly lucrative furniture-flipping business.

Anyhow, once in the store, James encouraged me to buy about a hundred dollars' worth of paint and wax, as well as a wax brush. This felt extravagant for us. I was trying to negotiate that it'd be for my birthday and Christmas. But James said I should just go for it—he felt that it would be a fun hobby, especially since we'd already driven all this way. I humbly bit the bullet and made the purchase.

The very next day, I knew I needed to get started painting something, for fear of feeling guilty about wasting our money on a whim. I decided to browse through the furniture section of Craigslist and find something under twenty dollars for sale in our area. Right away, I saw the ten-dollar table, which became so symbolic of my efforts. I sensed something was wrong with the table, but I contacted the seller and set a time for James to go look at it to see if it was salvageable.

The Origional Ten-Dollar Table

As soon as James got off work, he left to go check out the table. He met the owner at a storage unit, and apparently, there were two other ladies who were interested, and they met him there as well. The ladies immediately rejected it because they felt the piece was hopeless. The tablecloth, which had covered the surface of the table, had embedded a sticky, fuzzy goo into the top layer.

When James came home with the table, I saw it as a challenge. I was determined to get this thing looking like it came off a showroom floor, in no time. Where would I begin? The piece had to be stripped completely... Or did it?

The next morning, I saw the ugly brown table sitting on the back deck. It looked sad, and I was already getting ready to give up on the deal. I couldn't help but look at it through the window while I was washing dishes; it's like the table was calling to me. "Michele... Michele... You can't give up on me—why not make me beautiful again? What's the risk? I can't get any uglier."

I thought, "That's it... I'm not a quitter." I grabbed my block sander and hand-sanded the tabletop for about fifteen minutes, to remove the embedded fuzziness. After that, I dusted off the piece and started painting. I simply dipped my brush into the paint can, which was filled to the brim with a charcoal gray color, and I just let' er rip. Painting took me about a half an hour (it wasn't a very big table—see picture).

I let the paint dry for a couple of hours while I had a snack and played with the kids. Then, I went back to the porch and proceeded to wipe on the clear wax, buff the table out, and distress it a bit. Seriously, I had no idea what I was doing, but it felt all artsy-chic, and I was loving every second.

After a grand total of four hours, from start to finish, including snack/drying time, my masterpiece was finished. I was jumping up and down with joy because I knew this would sell. I mean, I really didn't even care if it did, though, because I liked it for my own house. Nonetheless, I immediately listed the piece on Craigslist. I posted it for $100, and within two hours, someone messaged me, to pick it up that evening.

The awesome thing is that I was able to paint, wax, and sell this now-gem of a table all prior to James getting home from work. I was able to have a hundred dollars cash, in hand, that night! It paid for all of my paint, and I still had paint and wax left to do enough furniture to fill a whole bedroom.

I was dying to paint everything in my house, and I became a true Craigslist junkie. Little did I know, James would become one, too.

INTRODUCTION

QUICK START

> "Never spend your money before you have earned it."
>
> Thomas Jefferson

Some of you have probably heard that you must spend money to make money. Well, there's some truth to that, but not entirely. You see, there are other things that equate to money, like time, services, and goods. I say this because I don't want you to read this chapter and think you'll need to invest money to start making money. In fact, I challenge you to begin this very week, without spending any money.

QUICK TIP

Begin this very week and start taking pictures of items in your house that you would like to sell.

After reading this Quick Start chapter, I'd like you to get up and start taking pictures of items in your house that you'd like to sell. This can be anything: an old statue or figurine, a piano, tea set, chairs, end tables, or anything else. Don't worry if they're not in perfect condition. Just take several pictures of items you're willing to give up—items you don't need anymore. Once you've taken several pictures in good lighting (preferably daylight), then you'll want to get measurements of the items.

Now, it's time to start listing these items. Price your items for a quick sell (meaning they sell in one to two days). Find similar items and see what they're going for in your area. Also, consider what you would pay if you bought these items brand-new in a store. Obviously, you'll want people to feel like they're getting a deal. Isn't that how we all want to feel?

Now, for the description on your listing, you'll want to make it enticing but realistic. Be honest about the condition, but don't overemphasize the negatives.

The following description will give you an example of how your listing could sound:

> ······ **LISTING SAMPLE** ······
>
> Gorgeous French-Cottage Style Sofa Table in a light gray-washed finish!
>
> We're selling this beautiful sofa table. It's in excellent condition and has a nice, clean gray-washed finish. This would be be a lovely addition to any home.
>
> Measurements 50" long, 18" wide, 29" tall

There are only two main elements to creating a classy listing: a minimum of four pictures (with natural lighting, not flash) and a proper description with measurements and price. Once you've done this a few times, and have had some buyer responses, then you'll start feeling like a professional. It's that easy!

One of the coolest things about selling furniture online (through Craigslist, Facebook Marketplace, OfferUp, Letgo, Mercari, Close5, eBay, and whatever other buy/sell apps, websites, and groups that are the most popular at the moment) is that you'll start having a lot more cash around. All my fellow furniture-flippers usually deal in cash. This was uncomfortable for me, at first. I was used to spending all of the cash I had in the house or in my purse. This mentality will not work with flipping furniture. You must learn to keep some cash from previous sales on hand, or else be prepared to pull cash out of your bank in a skinny minute (be thankful for ATMs) so you can jump on the next purchase.

There will be times when you'll have customers who will want to pay in different ways. Currently, cash seems to be the preferred method. Non-cash methods of payment, like Venmo and PayPal, are more common for higher-priced purchases. I imagine that, in the coming years, cash payments will fade away, but only time will tell. It's good to be prepared to take any form of payment from customers.

After selling the ten-dollar table, I went a little crazy, and so did James. We became full-fledged believers.

> **QUICK TIP**
>
> Look out for scams. Two of the most common red flags to look out for are buyers refusing to meet you or insisting on paying with personal checks or anything that requires a money transfer. It's best to deal in cash, PayPal, Venmo or something similar.

So, we did the next logical thing—we bought eighteen used restaurant chairs off of Craigslist for $80 (held back from the previous table sale) and started selling virtually all of the furniture in our house, from my daughter's desk to our old bedroom set and dining room set.

I basically turned our entire house into a showroom. This is not something I'd recommend to beginners, but it worked for us at the time. However, I would recommend turning one room in your house into a showroom. I like the idea of using your dining room or a first-floor bedroom or study. You can keep the room pretty and staged with your latest masterpiece, and then after you sell it, you can rotate in your next work of art. The fantastic part is that you'll have new and beautiful furniture rotated out weekly, so you'll never get tired of what you see in your house.

So, back to those restaurant chairs. Yep... James was super excited about the possibility of making lots of cash. I thought he'd gone slightly insane and couldn't believe he'd crammed eighteen chairs into the back of our old Chrysler minivan. It was like a mad game of Tetris. Those gaming skills ended up coming in handy for all of us.

The Restaurant Chairs
Minivans can be just as great for transporting funiture as trucks. We fit eighteen restaurant chairs in our minivan when we first started flipping furniture.

When he brought the chairs home, I quickly went to work on them. I cringed at the old gum and hair I had to pull from some of them (I'm kind of a germaphobe). I'd never reupholstered anything in my life, but I unscrewed the seat cushions and cut off the dirty pleather (imitation leather) on them in no time. Cutting old pleather is not for the faint of heart.

After much blood (literally), sweat, and tears, I quickly learned shortcuts and safety techniques that protected my hands from getting cut up. Simple reupholstering is fun, but aside from transporting pieces, it's, in my opinion, the most time-consuming and dangerous part of a furniture flip. Got to watch out for those staples.

Carefully fold and tightly pull the fabric so it looks smooth and professional. I'd recommend watching a few YouTube video tutorials beforehand so you don't have to learn lessons the hard way, like I did.

QUICK TIP
Do a search on Amazon for "damask shower curtains" to find inexpensive fabric.

Anyhow, the fun part is picking out fabric. Make

Offer Custom Options
Custom options are very attractive to customers, and you can boost your sales by offering contract or custom work. A great way to start is by offering a few different options for pieces you already have, like we did for these restaurant chairs.

sure you only use the cash from your previous sale when you pay for your fabric. Later, you can learn to leverage with credit cards, but I don't recommend this in the beginning.

The fabric store quickly became my new favorite place to shop—so many colors and designs. I can still lose track of time walking down the aisles, searching for a good deal that has the look I'm going for. Keep in mind, though, that your end-goal is to make a profit—so you'll always want to choose from the fabric styles on sale. There will be plenty of those to choose from.

So, back to those eighteen chairs. Initially, I started selling them too cheap. I posted a listing on Craigslist offering to customize them for only thirty-five to forty dollars a piece. I later learned that I could have gotten twice that amount if I had been a tad more patient. But I was a newbie, and I was super excited to make the sales. My inbox was flooded with emails from people wanting to purchase the chairs, which I offered in white or charcoal, with either a lovely toile fabric or a trendy red paisley fabric.

Who knew they would be so popular? Even at the steal-of-a-deal price I'd set, I ended up making about $600 profit, within two weeks. If I had priced them properly, I would've been able to make at least $1,000 profit. With more experience I also realized that chairs like that are even more valuable when paired with tables. The knowledge I gathered from those sales was priceless, and it set the stage for building relationships with customers for custom work. I wasn't mad at myself for losing $400, but rather considered it a lesson learned—and I did make a profit.

In the beginning, it would be wise to deal only in cash, but as you start to move in the direction of larger sales, like $800 dining room sets and $1,000 bedroom sets, then you may want to consider the option of invoicing your customers through an online platform like Venmo, PayPal, or Square. Many buyers will welcome the option of paying with a credit card, and you'll have the sale documented and backed up in case there are any problems getting the money in full.

Even with all of the technological advances we have for making payments these days, there is still something to be said about good old-fashioned, hard-earned cash that you can hold in your hand and count. Just remember, you can lose this stuff, and if you're like me, you're going to have to be very cautious about where you put it. Eventually, it will feel completely normal to be dealing with a couple of thousand dollars in cash. You'll have to decide what percentage is yours to spend on personal expenses, what will need to be reinvested into the business, and what should be saved in a bank account.

I hate to admit it, but there were a few times when several hundred dollars got misplaced because James and I just weren't accustomed to keeping track of cash. We ended up stashing it on top of our refrigerator so the kids couldn't accidentally find it, but I can't remember how many times I reached up there and felt nothing. Needless to say, I learned my lesson pretty quickly.

At first, you may just deposit your cash into your personal checking account, but that can make things a bit tricky when it comes tax time. Eventually, you'll come to the realization that it would be wise to open a separate bank account to deposit the money you receive from your business. This can be an additional personal account. It doesn't need to be a true bank-classified business checking account when you first start out.

In the beginning, it's good to put a high percentage of your sales back into your next furniture purchase. Later, once you build up a steady cash flow, you can adjust this. Remember, you can build your business as big as you like; all you must do is set your goals. As you'll see later in this book, it's possible to make a six-figure income by simply flipping furniture and other home decor items.

Once you envision the possibilities, I hope you will start to feel the excitement, like I first did and, to this day, still do. You can truly be your own boss and make your own hours. There's something so gratifying about being able to sleep in some mornings, and having others where you wake up early to a nice cup of coffee, grab a paintbrush, and get busy painting your next masterpiece. Talk about a wonderful creative outlet you can work around your schedule, all while bringing in a nice income. I could go on and on about this, but I'm sure your imagination can lead you to all of the possibilities. Don't be afraid to dream a little, but be careful! Furniture-flipping can become extremely addictive.

> **QUICK TIP**
>
> Get organized with your money. If you can, open another account to separate business income and expenses. This will help you plan better. Also, make sure to keep some cash on hand in a safe place.

FAST CASH JUMPSTART

6 STEPS TO GETTING STARTED TODAY

STEP ONE

Find items around the house you no longer want or need and take several close-up pictures in daylight.

STEP TWO

Look at selling sites and see how similar items are priced in your area. Compare and set your price.

STEP THREE

List your items for sale on a few online selling sites.

STEP FOUR

Price competitively to sell quickly.

STEP FIVE

All that's left to do after that is to wait for a bite and answer any questions people may message you with.

STEP SIX

Once the items are sold, you can use your profit as seed money to buy painting supplies and more furniture.

CHAPTER ONE

THE SNOWBALL EFFECT

> "Building wealth is a marathon, not a sprint. Discipline is the key ingredient."
>
> *Dave Ramsey*

We all want financial freedom, right? But most of us, at some time or another, have felt like Veruca Salt, in *Willy Wonka and the Chocolate Factory*, stamping her foot and yelling, "Where's my golden ticket? I WANT MY GOLDEN TICKET!" We simply don't have the patience or the discipline to earn our golden ticket humbly and forbearingly. Remember, your time will come, but every good thing starts small. Faith is critical, here, because there will be times when you want to get off course and may think your efforts are trivial. I'd like to encourage you to stay on the path. Don't be afraid to dream big, but you must start small. Just like the endearing Charlie Bucket, from the same story, let your humble beginnings be the fuel to your fire. Everybody has a dream! Let your dream grow into a reality.

That's all you need to begin flipping furniture: a dream... You don't need money to start, just a dream. As I said in the previous chapter, I don't want you to use any of your own money when you first start out. I want you to start selling a few small things (items in your home or storage facility that you no longer want or need) and use the cash from those sales to start investing in higher-end pieces.

When I first started, I stayed in the $200-or-under range. I tried buying things under fifty dollars and reselling them for around two hundred. I'd specifically pinpoint pieces with scratches, chips, and torn fabric on the seat cushions. I tried to steer clear of furniture with structural issues or complicated reupholstering. I could redo a simple seat cushion, but anything more than that was beyond my expertise.

So, you may ask, what types of furniture do you begin with? Well, that's up to you. Follow what you like and what you see people are really interested in buying. As time goes on, you'll understand the market in your area much better. In the beginning, it's good to get a wide array of items, from dressers, tables, and chairs for under fifty dollars. I learned that, in my neck of the woods in the Raleigh, NC, area, I could make the largest profit margin from flipping dining room sets. I usually tried to find four-to-six-chair dining room sets for between fifty and two hundred dollars, and I'd resell them for between three and eight hundred dollars. Second on my list was dressers and buffets (which required the least amount of work). Always remember, when searching for pieces online, what you see may not be impressive at all—it may be a bit disgusting like my eighteen restaurant chairs. Your job is to turn these pieces into real jewels—all it will take is some cleanup, paint, maybe waxing and buffing out, sometimes new fabric, or maybe just filling in some light scratches or chips. Eventually, you'll move on to the higher-end pieces, your money will "snowball," and you'll start to see it really accumulating. It'll seem like everything is accelerating, and you'll have more business and furniture inventory than you're capable of handling on your own. This is where your goals will need to come into play, here. You'll need to decide if you want to hire employees or eventually get a shop (you may never need a shop if you have enough space at your home or have some sort of garage to work in).

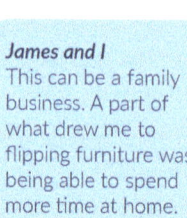

James and I
This can be a family business. A part of what drew me to flipping furniture was being able to spend more time at home.

The key is to keep investing your money back into new pieces (inventory for your customers), which starts with deciding what percentage of profit you want to make and how much you'll keep for reinvesting. In the beginning, you won't be able to keep much profit, but later, your profit margin will grow, especially as your haggling, painting, and staging skills grow.

You may ask, "How long will it take to get to a place where I can quit my day job?" My answer is that it can happen fast . . . maybe faster than you're prepared for. The key is to see if you are passionate about it. I was, and still am, for several reasons, extremely passionate about this business. I believe there are aspects of it that can appeal to almost anyone. For me, the most valuable part of this business is being my own boss, followed closely by the money, of course! The third and fourth reasons may not be your cup of tea, but they appeal to me, and I'm sure to many others: I love

QUICK TIP

Keep it simple and look for furniture that needs only minor work or no work at all… something you can turn around and stage properly in better lighting and resell for a profit. You'll want to jump on great deals as soon as you see them. There are some great apps that notify you when new listings are posted.

the decorating and staging aspect, as well as working with clients. I love seeing how happy people get when they buy a piece they are really thrilled about, and I can say I had a part in that.

Now, if you're not a people person, you can work toward hiring someone who is, and they can be the one who deals with customers and transports the furniture; you can be the artist, or vice versa. If you want to do the driving but do not have a big enough vehicle, you can rent one. If you like the thrill of finding a good deal but don't enjoy the painting, you can hire people to do the painting for you.

I like starting out with low overhead. I worked on my own in the beginning, handling pretty much everything, and James and I kept an eye out for a good deal every day. Currently, we spend a good thirty minutes a day scanning a couple of selling sites, and it's pretty fun! It feels like shopping for a deal. Now, who doesn't love that?

James and I have become a selling team. It makes me laugh because, honestly, decorating isn't his "thing" at all, but making money is. Now, he's learned to love the business almost as much as I do. He really enjoys the thrill of finding a good deal. Like I said, we became Craigslist junkies quickly when we first started. Our garage and home quickly became filled with more inventory than we could handle, and people started calling me right and left for custom work. I honestly couldn't keep up with it on my own without hiring someone else.

So, here is a simple and realistic picture of how rapidly things can grow.

THE SNOWBALL EFFECT

ONE EXAMPLE

WEEK ONE
You sell a few items from your home that you don't need anymore (an old dresser for $100, a couple end tables, and a decorative statue for $80).

WEEK TWO
You take $150 of the previous sale and purchase a dining room set with four chairs, plus a chalk finish painting kit that'll last you for several pieces of furniture. You pocket thirty dollars as your profit from Week One.

WEEK THREE
You list the dining room set you've spent a day painting and sell it for $350. Then, you reinvest $200 into a $50 dresser and a $150 dining room set with six chairs. You pocket a hundred dollars as your profit from Week Two sales.

WEEK FOUR
You do some simple touch-up work on the six-chair dining room set (from Week Three), and you list it with gorgeous staged photos. You get $580 from that sale and another $280 from the dresser you've repainted.

Let's stop and evaluate what just happened over the course of a month and only took you about twenty hours of actual work during those four weeks.

In this hypothetical example, in one month, you've managed to take a couple of items from your home that you didn't even want or need anymore, and you turn them into almost a thousand dollars' worth of profit. Just think of what you could do in the next four weeks. Let's use our imagination here. Check out the following example of Week Five through Week Eight. Your snowball is going to become colossal! You're going to be blown away!

> **QUICK TIP**
> Remember to hold back enough money to reinvest in more furniture and project supplies

WEEK FIVE

You pocket $400 from Week Four, and you reinvest $460 into paint supplies, a Duncan Phyfe-style eight-chair dining room set ($300), a buffet ($50), and an old solid wood, scratched-up vanity for $80. You end up either touching up, painting, or just staging and flipping those pieces and getting $720 for the dining room set, $280 for the buffet, and $250 for the vanity, which equals $1,250.

WEEK SIX

You pocket $700 from Week Five, and you reinvest $550 into paint supplies, two dining room sets, a dresser, and a gold baroque mirror. You update the baroque mirror by dry-brushing the gold with white chalk finish paint. You redo both of the dining room sets by painting and reupholstering them, and then you paint the dresser. You end up selling all of the items for $1,450 that week. You can see how quickly this can become a full-time job.

WEEK SEVEN

You pocket $900 from Week Six, and you reinvest $550 into paint supplies and two more six-chair dining room sets. In addition, you have a couple of customers you've now acquired who call you about redoing some of their furniture (an old buffet, a dresser, a coffee table). You resell the dining room sets you've touched up, staged, and taken awesome pictures of. You receive a total of $1,100 for them, and you receive another $400 for the contract work you did—for a grand total of $1,500.

WEEK EIGHT

You pocket $1,000 from the week before, Week Seven. From this profit, you reinvest $500 into paint supplies, another high-end six-chair dining room set, and a dresser. You also get a call from someone who wants you to help repaint their kitchen cabinets that week for $800. You resell the dining room set and dresser for a total of $850, and you get $800 from the kitchen cabinets. You receive $1,650 that week and pocket $1100 of it! Wow!

Let's stop and evaluate what just happened in this hypothetical example over the course of two months' time, with only thirty hours of actual work per week.

In your second month, you've managed to pocket $4,100! Now, that's impressive! What's even more exciting is that it can continue to grow. There is an endless supply of old furniture that you can recreate, stage, and flip.. The best part is that, even when the economy is bad, people still are looking to buy furniture from these online selling sites. They seem to thrive in a bad economy. From what I've seen, in an improving economy, many people see advantages in staying with the procedures they found or developed during the bad economy. They look for good, friendly service, as well as good products. Give them both.

The sky is the limit, my friend. You'll just have to decide what your financial goals are and what kind of cash flow you're looking for each week. Are you interested in working this full-time? Do you want to hire and train people to do the work for you? Is this just going to be a nice hobby that helps to pay for groceries, credit card bills, or your kid's college tuition? Whatever the case, you can make this fit your life and goals.

> **QUICK TIP**
> After a few months, you may want to transition into contract work to start networking in your community.

CHAPTER TWO

FLIP YOUR LIVING

> "Collect things you love, that are authentic to you, and your house becomes your story."
>
> *Erin Flett*

By the time you get to this chapter, my hope is that you will have already tested the waters a bit by painting your first piece of furniture or trying to sell a few items you have no use for anymore. Once you've tasted just a bit of how this business works, I have a feeling you're quickly going to learn just how inspired you can become. You may become so passionate about this business that you want to sell everything in your home and simply start over. I know, for some, the thought of getting rid of furniture is scary because you become attached to things. You obviously don't have to get rid of all your furniture like I did (remember, my enthusiasm was a little over the top), but you may find that the furniture you are creating and selling is nicer than the things you own. You can't keep it all.

I absolutely got carried away with the painting aspect, as well. Before long, everything I laid eyes on became a potential candidate for painting and waxing. Within the first few months, James and I ended up selling nearly all of our furniture on Craigslist. From that point, I ended up really being able to understand my style and come into my own. I began to collect some of my most prized pieces, like gold baroque mirrors, chairs, hutches, dressers, night stands, desks—you name it. What I found through this process is that, after painting a piece, you may become attached to it and not want to let go of it. I believe this happens because you invest your time and energy into a piece, so you sort of fall in love with it. You can't keep everything in your house, though, or you'll become a pack rat; instead of making a profit, you'll go in the hole.

Nonetheless, there will be some pieces that are worth keeping, at least for a while, because you treasure them so much and because you're proud of your beautiful work. I ended up using our formal dining room for my staging area. I painted in there, as well, making sure to use drop cloths on our hardwood floors so as not to spill paint on them. The garage was also an excellent option for painting when the weather was nice, or when a completed piece was taking up the dining room. For a couple of years, we didn't have a dining room set that was truly ours to keep. We always had temporary ones that were for sale.

I remember the reluctance I felt when I finally decided to sell our fancy dining room set that we'd bought brand-new. It was sentimental because James and I had bought it when we were newly married. After starting the painting business, though, I quickly realized we needed the dining room for staging, pictures, and rotating new pieces in to sell them.

If you don't have a garage, then you may want to turn one room in your house into a showroom where you rotate pieces in and out as you flip and sell them. A dining room, sun room, or office may work.

We basically had a new dining room set every week. Hutches, dressers, and mirrors were also rotated into the dining room. Rather than being chaotic, this process was perfect for me. It felt like I was getting the opportunity to live in a new picture out of a magazine every time something was sold. I could live out all of my decorating dreams!

I put something new in my dining room almost daily. Often, I'd wake up, get my cup of coffee in the morning, and just sit and enjoy my momentary dream room. I'd usually spend a good hour in that room every morning, taking staged pictures, looking at decorating boards on Pinterest for motivation, and scanning what was for sale, making some offers.

QUICK TIP

Want a wood finish, but the veneer is damaged? Pull off any loose pieces of veneer and lightly sand the area smooth. Fill any holes with wood filler. Let it dry and sand smooth again. You can then apply Retique It ® liquid wood in one of our many wood shades and finish it with the stain color of your choice to get a wood finish!

You may be wondering what sort of furniture I'd look for. Well, other than structural soundness, I seek out pieces with classic lines and tongue-and-groove drawers. Some people are drawn to more modern straight lines, like mission-style, but I gravitate to the curves you find in French provincial, Bombay, and Victorian-style furniture. I recommend finding your style niche and going in that direction, especially since these pieces will be in your home. Why not enjoy them while they're for sale?

It's also good to go with what you love because you'll gain knowledge more quickly that way. Later, you can branch out into styles you're not as familiar with, if you feel so inclined. I never did branch out much into modern styles because vintage was my general niche and seemed to encompass such a vast array of furniture for sale online.

As far as quality goes, you don't always have to buy solid wood pieces. Granted, solid wood is usually a plus, but I don't want you to steer away from veneer. Veneer gets a bad rap, but if you put some chalk finish paint, plus wax, on an old veneer piece, it will feel, and look, like a million bucks. Don't even worry if the veneer is coming up a bit. You can get some wood glue and repair it in a snap.

FLIPPING YOUR KITCHEN AND BATHROOM

There really aren't many things in your home that can't be completely transformed with a little paint. That's why I believe that, once you start getting in the groove of painting, you'll discover a myriad of things you'd like to change about your own house. Many people would love to have a brand-new kitchen or bathroom, but new cabinets and counters are pricey.

Guess what?

You can use chalk finish paint on your dated kitchen and get a new trendy kitchen of your dreams for a fraction of the price. Oh, and the best part—no sanding and no surface prep other than making sure the cabinets are clean. You can even use chalk finish paint on old Formica countertops. I personally love the look of countertops done in Renaissance Gothic Grey—it has that lovely soapstone look, like in old chemistry labs.

> **QUICK TIP**
>
> When painting countertops, the key is to water your paint down a tad with a tablespoon or two of water. Then use a dense foam roller and brush for your application so there will be no brush lines and the surface will dry nice and sleek. After the paint dries, lightly sand. You'll want to seal your countertops in two or three coats of a clear satin poly. I like Fiddes Hard Wax Oil or one of our Retique It ® top coats.

When I first started painting, we were renting our home. I couldn't test out painting on our own kitchen, but luckily, I had the opportunity to paint other people's cabinets. Let me just say, the only thing more gratifying than seeing how happy people are with their kitchen and bathroom transformations is being able to get paid for it by carrying out that transformation. You can make good money by painting cabinets, and it is just another avenue that furniture painting may take you into, if that's something you enjoy.

Kitchens are definitely more time-consuming than the average furniture flip, but there really isn't much cost involved. It's just labor-intensive and could take anywhere from a day to a week, depending on how fast you are and how big of a kitchen you are painting and refurbishing.

What's nice about painting in chalk finish paint is that you don't even have to take the cabinet doors off. On many of my kitchen flips, I just paint right over the hinges. This saves so much time, and the overall look is basically the same. You'll just need to make sure to use painter's tape so you have clean lines and protect your appliances.

CHAPTER THREE

PAINTING TECHNIQUES & SUPPLIES

> "If you love something, it will work.
> That's the only real rule."
>
> Bunny Williams

Okay, so we're getting down to the nitty gritty of "flipping." Before I get into all of the details, though, I want to remind you that this won't be like any job you've had in the past. You're going to love flipping and the freedom it brings. Simply put, it all comes down to grabbing a paintbrush. For your first piece, I don't even care if your paintbrush comes from the dollar store; I just want you to have enough courage to dip your paintbrush in the paint can and just do it! Have at it! Don't be afraid.

Just stay focused on the job at hand, which is to cover a piece of furniture in paint. I know this dive-right-in technique works because I've watched my kids do it, and somehow, they magically manage to paint a little side table or chair, and it looks great. Try not to be hyper- critical of your first piece. Then, you'll want to seal your paint in wax. Please don't panic when you hear the word "wax." I know it sounds foreign because nobody really waxes their hardwood floors anymore. Nonetheless, it's just like waxing a car. As Mr. Miyagi, in *The Karate Kid*, says, "Wax on... Wax off."

I'm suggesting this laid-back approach because I don't want you to overthink your way out of furniture-flipping. You may want me to lay out all kinds of rules about painting, but there really are no rules. It's not an exact science—it's an art you will develop, even as you think back to those art projects you did as a child. You know, remember that little kid who liked finger-painting and water-painting? They're still inside you.

> **QUICK TIP**
>
> Check out the FAQ section for more information on specific painting techniques and supplies.

Any skilled painter, no matter what age, needs some basic supplies. So, below is a list of my favorite supplies to have on hand for flipping furniture. Let me start by saying, I'm a big fan of chalk finish paint (you can use almost any paint for painting furniture, but I'll go into why I prefer chalk finish paint in the next chapter). I tested many different paints, looking for different brands to try and colors to match, and I became discouraged when I couldn't find a quick way to order any chalk finish color online.

Sometimes, if you want something done right, you must do it yourself. So, with James' help, I developed a way for people like myself to order any chalk finish paint color online, usually shipping within one to two business days. My team who has developed what I believe is one of the best chalk finish paints around. I've made it easy for customers to order any of our over forty popular colors, as well as choose a custom match of any color from a major brand.

My chalk finish paint brand is called Retique It ® by Renaissance Furniture and Cabinet Paint. Now, without further ado, the following is a list of basic supplies for flipping furniture

BASIC SUPPLIES

TO GET YOUR WORKSTATION STARTED

- One or two synthetic, angled, professional paintbrushes
- One 1-½ inch round wax brush with natural bristles
- Several inexpensive chip brushes in varying sizes
- Chalk finish paint in two or three neutral colors, including at least one shade of white and a gray or beige color
- Furniture wax—clear, dark, and white
- Polyacrylic—satin finish
- Latex gloves
- An apron
- Clean, lint-free socks for buffing out the wax

QUICK TIP

If this list overwhelms you, feel free to check out Retique It ® Chalk Finish Paint's Deluxe Starter Kit. This has all of the basic necessities for starting a furniture-flipping project.

CHAPTER FOUR

WHY CHALK FINISH PAINT

> "All you need to paint is a few tools, a little instruction, and a vision in your mind."
>
> Bob Ross

I'll make this short and sweet and sum it up in three major reasons. First, and most importantly, I love chalk finish because there is minimal surface prep and sanding required prior to painting. Most coatings require a primer application or heavy sanding prior to painting—and as Sweet Brown so eloquently stated,

"AIN'T NOBODY GOT TIME FOR THAT."

Sometimes, a little sanding, just to scuff the surface up, is fine. Roughing the surface up isn't time-consuming like sanding it completely down. Chalk finish paint removes the need to have to completely strip the old surface. Your time is valuable, and being able to do quality work quickly is important.

The second reason is that chalk finish paint is so versatile—you can use it on almost anything: old mason jars, furniture hardware, upholstery, pottery, you name it. You can even make almost anything into a chalkboard if you leave the painted surface unfinished. Chalk finish paint is versatile enough for modern or vintage furniture.

I love the look and charm of vintage furniture. I mean, like, I'm crazy about Jane Austen stories, all things BBC, and anything that reminds me of something mysterious from a distant time when men wore powdered wigs and makeup and women wore corsets. Hey, I don't want to go back to that time, I just think things were more beautiful and refined in the French Renaissance, Baroque period, and especially the Victorian era.

But I digress. My point is that chalk finish paint that is sealed in wax gives the most unique, aged look, which is hard to duplicate any other way. The wax adds the texture of polished wood. I can't even count how many times I've taken an old French provincial table covered in distasteful veneer, painted it with chalk finish paint, waxed it, and given it this high-end vintage look and feel. Yeah... this stuff is that good!

The third reason for using chalk finish paint is because it's eco-friendly and has little to no odor. When I first started painting, I had to paint in the house around my toddler. I never had to worry about the fumes of chalk finish paint bothering my young child. It felt good making such a wise choice in my product selection. When painting furniture becomes your job, open cans of paint become a way of life, and the house could quickly become filled with toxic fumes. This just isn't the case with chalk finish paint, though. To this day, I still take pride in knowing I'm selecting the best type of paint when it comes to the environment and my family's health. It's really a no-brainer to me.

A Family Affair
A crafternoon with the youngest of the Corwin children.

MICHELE CORWIN

SELECTING THE RIGHT COLOR

Most of the used furniture you purchase will probably be made with stained wood. You'll be faced with the decision of leaving it as is, painting it with a color, or painting it with a liquid wood coating (check out my chapter about Retique It ® liquid wood), which you'll need to stain. My advice, in the beginning, is to keep your cost down and only buy about three quarts of neutral colors. Buying several shades can quickly get expensive. When you see the pictures of many of the pieces I've redone, you'll see that I frequently used a few of the same colors. Hey... it sells!

I clearly remember that, after painting a couple of pieces in white and gray, I longed to be able to paint with vibrant colors like hot pinks, yellows, and oranges. There is something very satisfying about painting with bright colors, but here is what I quickly learned: Those. Colors. Don't. Sell. Quickly! Now, you're probably thinking, "How boring," and let me just say, there is a time and place for everything. You'll have your chance to be a kid in a candy store with colors, but it shouldn't be in the beginning.

The time for using vibrant colors is when you start doing custom and contract work. We won't dive deep into talking about contract work here, but the gist is that quickly, the word will get out that you flip furniture, and people will start calling you to paint the furniture they already own. Here is your chance to go bold. One example of this is when a customer requested that I paint her TV console/dresser in a bright green (the Retique It ® by Renaissance color is called Jade). If I remember correctly, she wanted it to match the felt on her pool table (fun!). And wow, did that green pop!

She absolutely loved the piece when it was all finished, and oh, how I enjoyed painting with that bright green color.

Now, if you're painting a piece strictly for yourself, then have at it. You can choose any color you like. But when it comes to furniture you're going to sell for a profit, I'd stick with neutrals, like shades of white, black, gray, brown, and beige. Navy blue can also be considered a classic color that is easier to sell. There will be times when you'll be able to sell a very light shade of blue or green, or a vintage red color, but for the most part, that will be the extent of what sells well. Obviously, trends may change, but sticking with classic colors will give you a larger market to whom you can appeal. Very few people will want a bright green dresser or a hot pink end table. Those flashy colors tend to narrow your market, and you could end up waiting months to sell something you could have sold in days. My little tip is that, if you want

to go bold, then do it with the hardware. Upgrading your hardware to crystal knobs or painting them in a metallic color can really jazz up your piece. Just think how much of a difference new hardware makes on kitchen cabinets.

> **QUICK TIP**
>
> When it comes to furniture that you want to sell for a quick profit, you'll want to stick with neutrals, like whites, grays, and wood tones. Vibrant colors should generally be reserved for custom pieces, per a client's request, or times when you're willing to wait for a buyer.

QUICK START GUIDE: CHALK FINISH PAINT

STEP ONE

Make sure the surface is squeaky clean. Use a multipurpose cleaner to spray the surface, and then wipe it down thoroughly with a clean cloth. Consider wiping the surface down with denatured alcohol if you're concerned it has some grease/wax/oil buildup. This will ensure that the surface will take the paint.

STEP TWO

Use a clean synthetic nylon/polyester brush for painting. Dip your brush into a cup of water to dampen it before dipping it into the chalk finish paint. Do this as often as needed to keep things smooth and flowing.

STEP THREE

Apply one to three coats of paint to achieve the look you're going for. See FAQ & Troubleshooting section at the end for detailed painting instructions and techniques. Allow paint to thoroughly dry for two to eight hours. The humidity level will affect the drying time. When allowing a piece to dry overnight, indoors is always a safe option.

STEP FOUR

Apply a sealer over your paint. You can apply a polycrylic, clear wax or a polyurethane. Please note: Polyurethane can cause white tones to turn yellowish in color (which is not usually desirable). Polyacrylic tends to be a better sealer for keeping super whites bright and yellow-free.

Check out this shabby chic look made by a customer using Retique It Chalk Finish Paint!

Photo Credit to Sheryl Marlee

Go to RetiqueIt.tv for video tutorials

CHAPTER FIVE

THE SECRET OF RETIQUE IT®

"Every artist was first an amateur."

Ralph Waldo Emerson

There are very few times a product has changed my life. However, Retique It ® liquid wood has changed mine, and it can change yours by taking your furniture-flipping business to a whole new level. I believe in it so much that James and I have partnered with its creator, to offer it to the public. I mean . . . I wish I'd had this magical substance when I first started flipping furniture because I could have made a ton of money with it. So, here's my little insider's tip: try Retique It ® liquid wood!

Here's why...

Retique It ® liquid wood is a revolutionary new eco-friendly paint made with real recycled wood—it's liquid wood! There is nothing else like it on the market, right now. It was patented in 2018. It comes in different shades of unfinished wood color and is basically liquid wood that you can paint onto almost any hard surface. You can paint it onto plastic, glass, cement... you name it. And best of all, you can paint it onto furniture and cabinets that have previously been painted. Seriously—no sanding or stripping off the old paint. You just paint it on and then stain it. You'll want to seal it after the stain dries, but that's basically it. It's just three main steps.

The awesome part is that you'll be able to give almost anything a gorgeous wood finish. It looks and feels like wood because it is wood. Retique It ® liquid wood uses breakthrough science that incorporates real recycled wood into a water-based paint that will actually absorb stain the same way that unfinished wood does. It's so much better than veneer and is as durable as the sealant you use. You can take a white dresser or tabletop and give it a dark walnut finish, a driftwood look, or even a beautiful gray stain. The possibilities are endless.

> **QUICK TIPS**
>
> Putting a new wood finish on tabletops, dressers, desks, etc. can dramatically increase their value with minimal effort when you use Retique It ® liquid wood.

Accent Wall
Getting the farmhouse plank look without all the cost using Retique It ® liquid wood.

Photo Credit: Amithy Eve Crawford

APPLICATIONS INCLUDE:

- Furniture
- Drywall
- Picture frames
- Cabinets
- Doors
- Concrete
- Fireplace mantels
- Hard flooring
- Wainscoting
- Window frames
- Exterior siding/trim
- Painted surfaces
- Crafts and decor
- And so much more!

QUICK TIP

Don't overlook non-wood furniture. With Retique It ® liquid wood, you can transform pieces that aren't even wood and give them a wood look as quickly as you can paint them! The process is simple, inexpensive, and doesn't require any carpentry skills or toxic chemicals.

QUICK TIPS

A Retique It ® liquid wood top, combined with a chalk finish painted base, gives a timeless look that is versitile and sells easily.

WHY I CHOSE RETIQUE IT ®

Retique It ® liquid wood is water-based, biodegradable, and low VOC, with no offensive smell or damage to our environment. Now, pieces that were once deemed unsalvageable can be given a brand-new wood finish. If you absolutely hate sanding down chairs and tabletops, then you are going to love this stuff.

Retique It ® liquid wood can be applied using an inexpensive paintbrush or paint sprayer by professionals and DIYers alike. Cleanup is as simple as using soap and water.

Retique It ® liquid wood allows you to skip the time-consuming step of stripping the old finish. Its adhesion and absorption properties are excellent, which allows your stain to absorb like it would on an unfinished wood surface. After applying Retique It ® liquid wood, you can use any manufacturer's stain and sealant to create the look and finish you want.

It's so easy to use.

Before I had Retique It ® liquid wood, clients would request a wood top, and I would panic because it made things more complicated, time-consuming, and sometimes impossible. Then, we discovered Retique It ® liquid wood, and it was a game changer for my business. I was able to offer more without sacrificing all of my time sanding and stripping to get a clean wood look.

Three steps is all it takes.

Paint It - Stain It - Seal It
LOVE IT!

THE SECRET OF RETIQUE IT

FOUR WAYS TO BOOST YOUR BUSINESS

WITH RETIQUE IT ® LIQUID WOOD

ONE
Save time. You'll save several hours sanding or stripping to get a wood finish. People will pay more for a high-quality, unblemished wood look.

TWO
It's super durable. You can use a poly right over it for a super durable finish. This is perfect for flipping tables, desks, and dressers that get a lot of wear and tear.

THREE
Use it on more than just furniture. It's great for transforming cabinets and old floors—cement floors, too. You can save your clients thousands of dollars and save yourself so much time and effort. You don't have to be a skilled carpenter to give your clients a new kitchen or wood flooring.

FOUR
Repair surface damage like watermarks, rings, and surface scratches. Some larger scratches can be repaired by allowing Retique It ® liquid wood to pool in the area of concern and allow several hours for the entire surface to dry before staining.

MICHELE CORWIN

QUICK START GUIDE: RETIQUE IT®

STEP ONE

Clean surface and allow to completely dry. You will need to remove severe chipping or peeling by lightly sanding. This will give a solid and stable base for Retique It® liquid wood to adhere to.

STEP TWO

Apply Retique It® with a paintbrush or paint sprayer using long, even strokes. Allow up to two hours to dry. Use soap and water to clean up drips and spills. Fill in any holes, divots, or deep scratches with non-silicone filler before applying Retique It® liquid wood to get the smoothest application.

USE A GRAINING TOOL AND A SECOND LAYER OF RETIQUE IT® LIQUID WOOD IN A DIFFERENT COLOR FOR A PROMINENT GRAIN.

····STEP THREE···················

Apply stain or paint to obtain the desired finish. To give a deep grained effect, you may consider applying an additional application of Retique It ® liquid wood and pull a graining tool through it in long, even strokes while it is still wet. Once dry, you can apply a stain color of your choice or even layer stains for a custom look.

LINOLEUM TILES ARE GREAT TO PRACTICE ON!

···NOTE···························

Try using dark over light Retique It ® liquid wood to get a more defined, rustic grain. You can also do light wood over dark wood Retique It ®. The possibilities are endless!

·····STEP FOUR·····

Apply a top coat such as polyurethane to protect the finish. I like to use Fiddes Hard Wax Oil in satin for surfaces that get a lot of wear and tear. While durable, some polyurethanes and Fiddes can yellow white- or gray-toned wood. For light colors, consider using Retique It® Polyacrylic.

Go to RetiqueIt.tv for video tutorials

Retique It liquid wood references a restorative product sold by Renaissance Innovations LLC which is a liquid product that contains 11% emulsified wood by weight, and is 66% wood by volume. Retique It®, the content in this book, and any trademarks referenced in this book are not associated with, nor is such content endorsed by, the trademark LIQUIDWOOD®, or its owner Abatron, Inc.

CHAPTER SIX

STAGING, LIGHTING, & PHOTOS

"Simplicity is the ultimate sophistication."
Leonardo da Vinci

This section is so critical. The guidelines I'm about to share can literally make your profit go up by hundreds of dollars on just one single furniture listing, if you follow them correctly. This all may sound basic at first, and you may think, surely, anyone would know this stuff. But clearly, people don't, as you can see by browsing the current listings on various sales media.

Take a good look at the competition out there. Scroll through the offers for grins and chuckles. I always get a few laughs every time I look through the listings. For example, let's say I see an ad for a disassembled dining room table. There might be only one poorly lit picture of it in a storage unit, and the person is asking $1,000 for it. I wouldn't pay $1,000 for something I can't see. And unless the storage unit was nearby, I would be unlikely to take the time and trouble to go out and see the table.

Would you expect that anyone else would want to, either? Seriously, you can easily distinguish between the people who have done this before and the ones who are amateurs. I've seen some of the worst attempts to sell a piece of furniture. Sometimes, the pictures are even upside down. This has worked to my benefit because sometimes there is a gem to be found where few would dare to look—nobody else gives those pieces a second look, and the seller is often willing to offer you a better deal.

Sure, anyone can take a picture. Many of us become masters at taking a stellar selfie. So, think of this like a selfie. You want to put your best foot forward. Just like, on social media, you wouldn't want to post a selfie taken in the middle of the night, in bad lighting, with your hair all wild. Likewise, you don't want to take pictures of your furniture at night or in a dirty garage with a bunch of assorted junk in the background. Check out the following...

SEVEN GUIDELINES

FOR GETTING STELLAR PICTURES

ONE
Simplicity is key. This goes for both staging and equipment.

TWO
Use things you have on hand for staging.

THREE
Fresh flowers, or something green, goes a long way.

FOUR
Great lighting is everything

FIVE
The more pictures, the better—camera angles and perspective matter.

SIX
Keep it clean and neat.

SEVEN
Don't make it look too "commercial."

> **QUICK TIP**
>
> Simplicity goes for equipment, as well. Don't overinvest in camera equipment when most smart phones have cameras that will suffice. Unless photography is also a hobby of yours, you will waste more time trying to learn how to use specialized equipment than it's worth. Remember, time = money!

SIMPLICITY IS KEY

Try to think about what you'd be looking for when purchasing a used item online. You'd want to be able to see the item you're considering purchasing clearly. In other words, the object you're selling should be the focal point in the picture. You're not out to create photographic art—a table with flowers is sufficient. So, you should only use one or two props for staging. Try to keep the kids and pets out of the photo. Sure, they're cute, but just a tad distracting.

Another thing to consider is the surroundings. Consider taking pictures of your furniture indoors, on flooring that contrasts well with the color of the featured piece. You want your piece of furniture to really pop. You may need to invest in an inexpensive dark, or light, rug to make your piece stand out. White furniture against a light floor, or dark furniture against a dark floor, can appear drab and boring. The rug will be a simple fix to make your piece of furniture stand out, so you can get it sold fast.

USE ITEMS YOU HAVE ON HAND FOR STAGING

Staging can be simple and inexpensive. Throughout this whole book, my goal is to show you that you don't have to spend much at all for this business. I can almost bet you have several items that would be perfect for staging. Try to take a mental inventory of any items you have on hand that could double as props for staging.

> **PROPS FOR STAGING**
>
> - Pretty porcelain or glass bowl
> - Beautiful vase
> - Fresh fruit (lemons, limes, apples, oranges)
> - Candles/candleholders
> - Old assorted or leather-bound books
> - Elegant lamp

STAGING, LIGHTING, & PHOTOS

Now, I don't expect that you will have all of these things, but you may have a few, and that is enough to get started. You can build your collection of staging props as time goes on, as you see items for sale that you'd want in your home anyway (two birds with one stone). You can get a variety of looks from just a handful of items.

> **...QUICK TIP...**
>
> If fresh flowers aren't easily accessible or something you want to maintain, consider getting a natural-looking set of artificial flowers, like the tulips and lavender I used for staging throughout this book.

FLOWERS AND GREENERY GO A LONG WAY

At some point, you may just want an excuse to buy fresh flowers for your home. Fresh flowers and green potted plants do so much to brighten up a piece of furniture and make it feel brand-new. Any type of flowers will do, but I personally love buying Alstroemeria (aka Peruvian Lily or Lily of the Incas) for staging furniture. These flowers can be found at almost any local grocery store, and they are very inexpensive. I've found that they last a long time when compared to other flowers. So, you'll get more bang for your buck with these, and they come in a variety of colors. Flowers and green plants are great for a simple centerpiece, especially for dining room tables and dressers. They add a nice touch, making the piece of furniture look special.

GREAT LIGHTING IS EVERYTHING

Natural lighting is best for taking pictures. You want a potential buyer to think of your furniture as fresh, clean, and bright, not dark and drab, like you have it locked away in some dungeon. If you end up finishing a piece of furniture at night, please resist the temptation to take pictures for your listing with flash. You'll want to wait until the next morning (or the brightest part of the day for whichever room the furniture is in) to take all of the pictures. I don't believe anything can compare to natural lighting — not even the best filter out there for editing your pictures.

You'll want to be careful when using filters because some of them can change the appearance of the color of your piece. For example, there's nothing worse than someone driving all the way out to purchase a piece of furniture you have for sale, and then they decline because they thought the gray table was a blue-gray and not a beige-gray. Some camera filters can alter the coloring so much that a piece can become almost unrecognizable. So, just be careful to keep it real, but bright, and your buyers will thank you. Your pictures should be so clear that there should be no questions as to what is for sale. Eventually, you will get so good at taking pictures that you may have people buying your furniture without seeing it in person. This happens all the time if buyers love a piece of furniture and are afraid the item will sell before they have a chance to pick it up.

THE MORE PICTURES, THE BETTER

Camera angle and perspective matter.

Less is not more when it comes to the number of pictures. The more pictures you can take, the better. The goal is to take so many good pictures that the person interested will know exactly what they are buying and have no doubts or additional questions.

> **QUICK TIP**
>
> Make sure to point out the details, especially in pieces you are trying to sell as a set. When flipping this bedroom set, I used gold accents to make the ornate handles and details stand out.

Each picture should show a unique angle or detail of the piece. Most of your pictures should be shot from a low perspective—"shoot from the hip" style. I like to tell people to give their camera to a five-year-old and see their perspective through the pictures they take. That is the height—from the ground up—you should be shooting from. Your first instinct will be to shoot from your eye level. The majority of your pictures need to be what I call "shorty" pictures.

It's also great to do close-up pictures. If the furniture has fabric, you'll want to do a close-up of the fabric for one of the pictures. If the furniture has some sort of wood grain, or a unique finish, or intricate details, then you'll want to zoom in and get a close-up picture of that, as well. Including more pictures in your listing conveys that the item you're selling has value and is special. The additional pictures will give information that cannot be conveyed properly through words alone.

You may be wondering how many pictures are necessary. I usually recommend somewhere between four and twelve pictures. Some of the selling sites will limit the number of pictures to just a few, and on those, I'd recommend posting the maximum allowed. However, most of them will allow for more than just a few.

KEEP IT CLEAN AND NEAT

This almost goes without saying, but it's imperative that you keep the background of your pictures clean and neat. That means: pick up the drop cloths, paintbrushes, and trash. You can often get a couple hundred dollars more for a piece of furniture if you post pictures with a nice, clean background. Remember, you're not just selling a piece of furniture, you're selling a feeling and a look. If the pictures give off a messy or dirty vibe, potential buyers will associate the piece of furniture with its surroundings. This is even more critical when selling shabby-chic pieces.

I did some experimenting with this when I flipped some distressed-looking dressers and dining room tables. I did one listing with a garage-floor background and another that was staged in natural lighting in my dining room. The offers with the garage background consistently came in at several hundred dollars lower than when the pieces were photographed with a clean background, indoors, in natural lighting.

If you don't have a nice room to stage your furniture in, don't fret. You can stage an area outdoors or in your garage, just so long as the lighting's good and it looks like it's in a home, not a furniture showroom or yard sale. One way of creating this effect is by buying some discontinued hardwood/laminate flooring or an inexpensive rug to put under your piece. Wall paneling painted white or wallpaper in a trendy pattern can be used for the background. Get creative, but keep it inexpensive. Don't go too far in the other direction and do what James and I did in the next guideline.

Taken with my camera phone circa 2016

Below:
Piece of furniture before flipping. Note that, while this has natural light, it is coming from behind and produces too much glare.

Left:
Completed piece. Photo taken with my camera phone and simple staging.

MICHELE CORWIN

DON'T MAKE IT LOOK TOO "COMMERCIAL"

You don't need to make your pictures look like they're from a magazine or an Amazon listing with a white background (unless you're actually selling them on Amazon or Etsy). I didn't understand this at first, and James and I unfortunately invested in expensive lighting and drop cloths. This was a huge waste of money. What we learned, after our idea of commercial-style staging flopped, is that people want to feel like they are buying from an individual, not a store. They want to see what the furniture looks like in a real house like theirs.

Potential buyers expect the listing to look like you're selling something from your home. The furniture we tried to sell with a white background, using drop cloths, looked too professional, and we got very few bites. We quickly learned that special photography and lighting are not necessary—all you need is a good camera phone.

> **NOTE**
>
> Taking good photos of the furniture is as important as picking and "gussying up" the furniture. The photos are the initial impression a potential buyer will have of the item. If the photos don't do their job, the process will end without a sale. The tips below explain the process and how a minor error in photography might produce a major problem.

TAKING A PHOTO WITH FLASH

A flash might produce what seems like a good picture, but if the color is changed, even slightly, that is enough to give the buyer the wrong impression. Flash can also produce an unattractive and distorting glare that can flatten details.

TAKING A PHOTO WITH INDOOR LIGHTS

Indoor lights are different than sunlight and generally produce an unappealing yellow tone that can distort the color of your piece. A good camera may have settings and filters to let you use indoor light. But most of us do not have the technical ability with photography, let alone the expensive camera, to photograph furniture with indoor lights. In addition, a photo that looks like it was taken by a professional photographer may turn off some potential buyers and get them thinking you're not being genuine. Professional pictures, with white backgrounds, are only necessary if you're selling on sites like Etsy and Amazon.

TAKING A PHOTO WITH NATURAL LIGHT & STAGING

Use mother nature to light your piece when you can. Place the piece in an area with a lot of natural light or even outside if you don't have a lot of natural light indoors. Don't just show a blank piece of furniture. Let the buyer see how it can be used. You are selling the feeling just as much as you are selling the piece itself. I would recommend taking several photographs of each item from different angles. Blow them up on your computer; see which will look best printed out or on the websites you plan to use.

TUTORIAL ONE

VICTORIAN-INSPIRED DINING ROOM SET

VICTORIAN-INSPIRED DINING ROOM SET

BEFORE

This piece was obviously beautiful once upon a time, but instead of trying to keep with the darker wood tones, I decided to lighten this piece up by painting the chairs and table base in a bright white color (Retique It ® by Renaissance color Snow). I wanted to give the table a whole new rustic farmhouse vibe by doing the top in a heavy grained wood with gray undertones. I also searched out the perfect shower curtain to use as my fabric for reupholstering the dining room chairs. I like to find my fabric first before committing to the paint colors. This helps me find my color inspiration.

I LOVE THESE CLAW FEET!

PREP WORK

Due to the heavy flaking and nature of the varnish, properly prepping this piece was essential. I lightly sanded the flaking surfaces and dusted off excess residue. Then I thoroughly cleaned the table and chairs with denatured alcohol, being careful to remove any loose areas of varnish.

YOU WILL NEED

- Retique It ® Carbon Gray Kit
- Retique It ® Chalk Finish Paint in Snow
- Retique It ® Professional Brush
- Staining Cloth or Sponge
- Retique It ® Polyacrylic
- Stain-Blocking Primer
- Fiddes Hard Wax Oil

RETIQUE IT CARBON GRAY KIT

TUTORIAL: VICTORIAN-INSPIRED DINING ROOM SET

·· STEP ONE ··········

After completing the prep work, you can jump right in. Start by selecting your fabric and removing each seat cushion. I use the fabric selection to determine the color palette for the project.

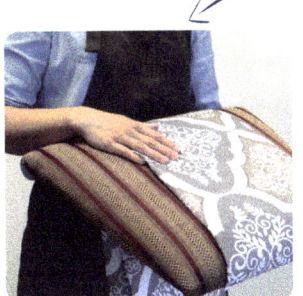

THIS IS A SHOWER CURTAIN!

··STEP TWO··········

Use a stain-blocking primer to give the chairs and base of the table a protective coat. This will prevent the red-toned lacquer from bleeding through when it is painted white. The top of the table will be done in Retique It ® liquid wood so it does not need a primer.

USE THIN COATS SO YOU DON'T LOSE ANY OF THE ORNATE DETAILS

·· STEP THREE ··········

Paint the chairs and the base of the table using the color Snow by Retique It®. Using a sprayer can help you speed things up and give you an even finish. I generally finish one chair completely to make sure the color and fabric work before doing all 8. Seal the paint with Retique It ® Polyacrylic or another non-yellowing poly.

MICHELE CORWIN

STEP FOUR

The table top is done using the Retique It ® Carbon Gray Kit. It includes a pint of Light Wood for the base, a half pint of Dark Wood for graining, Carbon Gray stain, a professional nylon paintbrush, a graining tool, gloves, and a rag. Stir the Retique It ® Light Wood well, until it has a smooth, paint-like consistency. Then use the brush to paint a thin coat in long, even strokes in the direction you want the grain.

ANY SYNTHETIC PAINTBRUSH WILL WORK!

STEP FIVE

Once the base coat of Light Wood is completely dry, it is ready to be grained with a coat of Dark Wood. Paint one section at a time and immediately grain it by sliding the graining tool along the wet area, rocking it slowly to get variation in your grain. Wipe away any excess product from the graining tool as you go. Repeat this for the entire tabletop, making long, plank-like sections.

  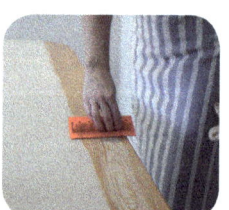

IF YOU DON'T LIKE THE GRAIN OF A SECTION ON THE FIRST PASS, YOU CAN EASILY GO OVER IT AGAIN WHILE IT IS STILL WET!

TUTORIAL: VICTORIAN-INSPIRED DINING ROOM SET

STEP SIX

Make sure all the grained sections are dry to the touch. Use a staining sponge to spread a thick coat of stain onto the surface in the direction of the grain, then wipe it away until you get an even color. For a deeper color, let the stain sit longer. Don't forget to get any ridges on the edge as well.

KEEP AN EXTRA RAG ON HAND FOR EASY CLEAN UP AND WIPING

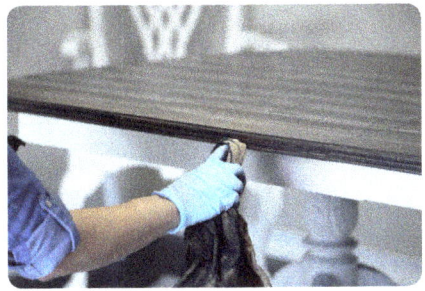

STEP SEVEN

Let the stain dry overnight. Make sure it is completely dry and not sticky or tacky to the touch before you attempt to seal it. If the stain is not thoroughly dry when you apply the protective coat, you may pull up some of the Retique It ® liquid wood and stain. Apply the protective top coat. I used Fiddes Hard Wax Oil on this tabletop for durability.

MICHELE CORWIN

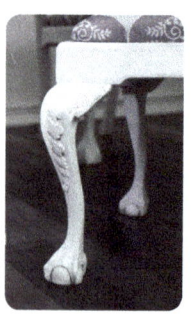

AFTER

This refinished dining room set has a farmhouse-chic vibe, so I paired it with simple-yet-elegant whites, a rustic galvanized tin pitcher, porcelain, and pops of greenery. The neutral wood tones and fresh décor allow the potential client to visualize this piece as a lovely addition to their own home.

TUTORIAL: VICTORIAN-INSPIRED DINING ROOM SET

TUTORIAL TWO

FRENCH PROVINCIAL DRUM TABLE

FRENCH PROVINCIAL DRUM TABLE

Before

I saw this piece from afar at a local thrift shop, and its peculiar design intrigued me. So, I snatched it up because it was on sale. I loved its fancy curves. As soon as I got home, I started researching what this piece was and soon found it was a drum table. I could almost imagine setting two French provincial chairs beside it for tea. I decided to give this piece a modernized facelift by getting away from the yellowish tones and moving into crisp white, with an ebony stained wood top. I also changed the brass hardware to vintage silver.

The extra storage space is an added bonus!

PREP WORK

While outdated and yellowed, this piece was still in fairly good condition with only minor wear and tear. I wiped it down with denatured alcohol and lightly sanded the top to shake off any of the loosened segments of veneer.

You Will Need

- Retique It ® Bleached Wood
- Retique It ® Chalk Finish Paint in Snow
- Retique It ® Professional Brush
- Ebony Stain
- Staining Cloth or Sponge
- Retique It ® Polyacrylic
- Rub'nBuff ® in Pewter

·· STEP ONE ··

Remove and clean all hardware, setting any screws aside in a safe place. I liked the shape and look of the current knobs, so I elected to keep them and update the color. Apply a small squeeze of Rub'nBuff ® directly onto the hardware and spread evenly using a cloth or gloved finger. Be careful not to overwork it, or you will pull the color up and have to add more product.

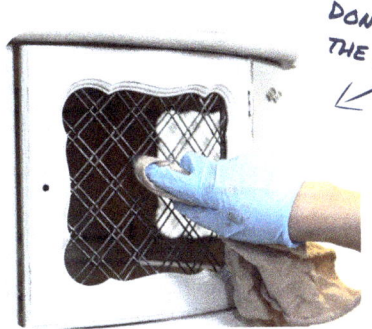

DON'T FORGET THE NETTING!

·· STEP TWO ··

Since this piece was in good condition to start, no primer was needed after a thorough cleaning. Using a damp brush, apply the paint in uniform strokes. If you start getting streaks or overly visible brushstrokes, re-dampen your brush.

MICHELE CORWIN

STEP THREE

Stir the Retique It ® Bleached Wood well, until it has a smooth, paint-like consistency. Then use the brush to paint a thin coat in long, even strokes in the direction you want the grain. Make sure to get the edges and under the visible areas of the lip. Repeat this for two to three coats, letting each layer dry thoroughly.

I LIKED THE CRACKLED TEXTURE OF THE ORIGINAL TABLE, SO I ONLY USED TWO THIN COATS IN ORDER TO LET IT COME THROUGH SOME.

STEP FOUR

Once the Retique It ® liquid wood is completely dry, use a staining sponge to spread a thick coat of stain in the direction you want the grain, wiping it away until you get your desired color. Let the stain dry overnight, then apply a sealer. For this piece, I used Retique It ® Polyacrylic for both the top and the painted areas.

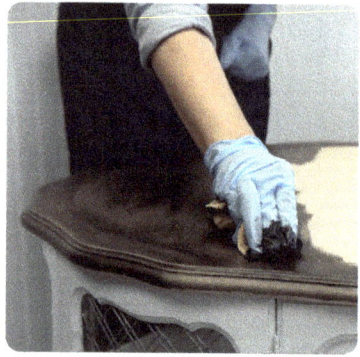

AFTER

Adding a wood top brought a refined, farmhouse-chic vibe to the piece without sacrificing its elegant, French provincial charm. The bright white gives it a neutral look that will attract more clients because of its versatility and ability to brighten up almost any space. This is definitely a conversation piece!

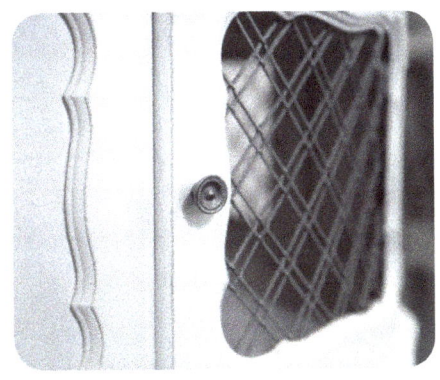

TUTORIAL THREE

ORNATE VINTAGE BEDROOM SET

ORNATE VINTAGE BEDROOM SET

Before

The ornate details of these two pieces made them a great match. I found them at a local, charity-based secondhand store as two separate pieces. Taking the time to envision what kind of customer would want to purchase this full headboard and chest of drawers was important in my color selection for the flip. I could see it in a lady's bedroom or little girl's room, so I picked a Retique It ® by Renaissance color called Cherry Blossom. I also wanted to give this set a lavish feel by adding some Grecian gold to the hardware and details of the headboard.

PREP WORK

These pieces had some flaking and wear, so I lightly sanded the surfaces and brushed off any excess or loose areas. Then I thoroughly cleaned each piece with denatured alcohol, being careful to smooth down any chipping and double-checking the drawers for any issues. Darker pieces like these may have bleed through and require a stain blocking primer.

You Will Need

- Retique It ® Light Wood
- Retique It ® Chalk Finish Paint in Cherry Blossom
- Kona Stain
- Retique It ® Professional Brush
- Staining Cloth or Sponge
- Retique It ® Polyacrylic
- Retique It ® Gold Wax
- Rub'nBuff ® in Grecian Gold

⋯ STEP ONE ⋯

Remove and clean all the hardware, setting any screws aside in a safe place. Apply a small squeeze of the Rub'nBuff ® directly onto the hardware and spread evenly using a cloth or gloved finger. Be careful not to overwork it, or you will pull the color up and have to add more product.

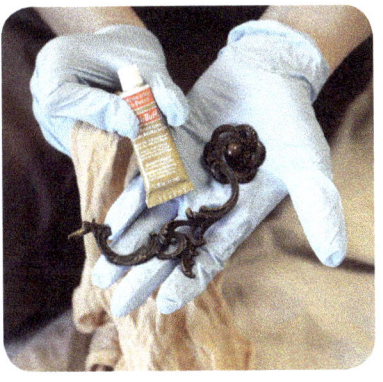

⋯ STEP TWO ⋯

Start with the bed frame. Paint each piece with Retique It ® by Renaissance Furniture Paint in Cherry Blossom. After you paint one piece, set it aside to dry while you paint the other. Repeat this for two to three coats. Set both pieces aside in a safe place.

MICHELE CORWIN

··STEP THREE··

Stir the Retique It ® Light Wood well, until it has a smooth, paint-like consistency. Then use the brush to paint a thin coat in long even strokes in the direction you want the grain. Wipe any dripping areas with soap and water.

··STEP FOUR··

While you let your first layer of Retique It ® dry, go ahead and remove the drawers of the dresser and start painting them in the same Cherry Blossom color used to paint the bed frame. Make sure to keep a cup of water on hand to dip your brush. This prevents streaks or visible brush strokes so you get an even finish. While you let the drawers dry paint the top with a second layer of Retique It ® Light Wood. Repeat until you have two coats of paint on the dresser and two coats of light wood on the top.

STEP FIVE

Once the paint and the liquid wood are both fully dry, tape off the top of the dresser. Using a rag or a staining sponge, apply a generous layer of the kona stain, wiping away any excess. Make sure you apply the stain in the same direction you applied the liquid wood. Let dry overnight.

STEP SIX

Once the bed frame is completely dry, apply an even coat of clear wax, buffing with a rag to get an even coverage over the entire surface. To bring out the ornate details and tie the colors back to the dresser, I decided to add gold wax. Take a natural bristle brush or rag and lightly brush over the raised details. Buff out any texture or chunks of wax. I wanted a vintage look, so I buffed some areas more heavily to give the piece a naturally aged look.

IT DOESN'T HAVE TO BE PERFECT. SMALL IMPERFECTIONS ADD TO THE VINTAGE LOOK!

STEP SEVEN

Going back to the dresser, make sure it is completely dry, not sticky to the touch, before attempting to seal it. If the stain is not thoroughly dry when you apply the protective coat, you may pull up some of the Retique It ® liquid wood and stain. Apply the protective top coat. I used Retique It ® Polyacrylic to seal the wood top and clear wax to seal the remainder of the dresser.

After

The soft pink creates a distinctly feminine look that specific buyers will jump on immediately because it looks very custom and can't be found in stores. Pair mismatched items and make them look like a set by giving them all a matching color scheme. Advertising sets like this can get you contract work overnight!

TUTORIAL FOUR

VERSATILE CONSOLE TABLE

VERSATILE CONSOLE TABLE

BEFORE

At first, I almost overlooked this piece because it had a heaviness to it (literally and visually), that dark "ugly wood" feel. In fact, to be honest, this piece smelled. I knew it wasn't beyond repair, and I could still envision it completely transformed in a different color. I wanted to make it neutral, so it could fit in a dining room, living room, or foyer.

PREP WORK

While this piece had good "bones," it also came with a less-than-desirable smell that quickly filled the room when the cabinets were opened. Most of the prep work for this piece was making sure nothing was growing inside it!

Tea tree oil is a great natural alternative to bleach for killing mold

You Will Need
- Retique It ® Bleached Wood
- Retique It ® by Renaissance Chalk Finish Paint in Alabaster
- Retique It ® Professional Brush
- Antique White Stain
- Weathered Gray Stain
- Staining Cloth or Sponge
- Retique It ® Polyacrylic
- Rub'nBuff ® in Pewter
- Retique It ® Clear and White Wax

STEP ONE

Remove and clean all the hardware setting any screws aside in a safe place. Apply a small squeeze of the Rub'nBuff directly onto the hardware and spread evenly using a cloth or gloved finger. Be careful not to overwork it, or you will pull the color up and have to add more product.

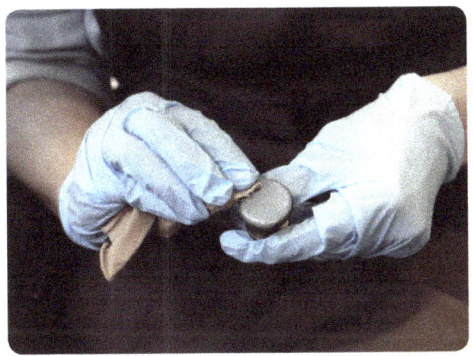

YOU CAN USE THE SAME TUBE OF RUB'NBUFF FOR MULTIPLE PROJECTS!

STEP TWO

Use a stain-blocking primer to give the base of the table a protective coat. This will prevent the red-toned lacquer from bleeding through the Alabaster paint.

MICHELE CORWIN

···STEP THREE···

Using a damp brush, apply a coat of Retique It ® chalk finish paint in Alabaster. Apply in uniform strokes, pushing into the grooves and crevices. If you start getting streaks or overly visible brush strokes, re-dampen your brush. Repeat for two to three coats.

···STEP FOUR···

Start by applying a coat of clear wax as a base, buffing out until it is smooth and your surface is fully covered. Using a natural bristle detail brush, add white wax to the ridges and edges, gently buffing out to give the piece a textured vintage feel. White wax is a great way to age a piece while keeping it visually light and bright.

One can of wax goes a long way and through multiple projects

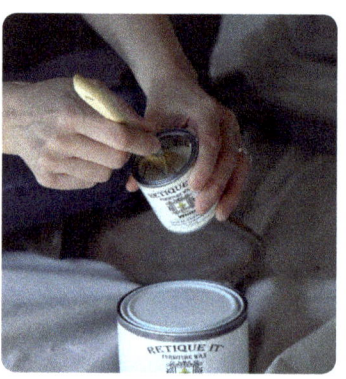

TUTORIAL: VERSATILE CONSOLE TABLE

⋅⋅STEP FIVE⋅⋅

Stir the Retique It ® Bleached Wood until it has a smooth, paint-like consistency. Then use the brush to paint a thin coat in long, even strokes in the direction you want the grain. Cover the surface completely and repeat for two coats, letting it dry fully between each application. Once the base coat is completely dry, use dark wood to paint one section at a time and immediately grain it by sliding the graining tool along the wet area, rocking it slowly to get variation. Repeat this across the entire tabletop.

MAKE SURE TO FREQUENTLY CLEAN THE GRAINING TOOL

DON'T FORGET THE EDGES!

MICHELE CORWIN

STEP SIX

Make sure all the grained sections are dry to the touch. Apply a wash of the Antique White stain, quickly wiping away to bring out the pink undertones of the dark wood. Let the the first layer of stain dry fully, then use a brush to spread a thick coat of the Weathered Gray stain onto the surface in the direction of the grain. Wipe away until you get an even color. For a deeper color, let the stain sit longer.

USE A THIN COAT AND WIPE QUICKLY FOR A WHITE WASHED LOOK

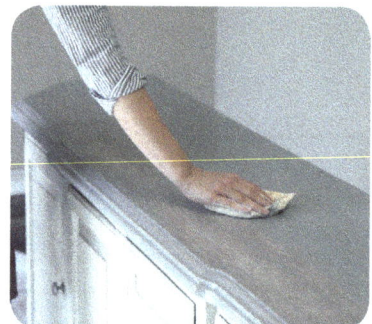

STEP SEVEN

Let the stain dry overnight. Make sure it is completely dry, not sticky or tacky to the touch, before attempting to seal it. If the stain is not thoroughly dry when you apply your protective coat, you may pull up some of the Retique It ® liquid wood and stain. Apply a protective top coat. For light-colored wood, like on this piece you will want to make sure you use a non-yellowing poly like Retique It ® Polyacrylic.

AFTER

Even though this piece is very large, it no longer feels overpowering because of the lighter grays. The addition of the wood grain on top adds some uniqueness and a high-end feel without being too dramatic. This piece would be beautiful in a beach house, cute little cottage, or any home with traditional style home décor.

TUTORIAL FIVE

SETTING UP YOUR WORKSTATION

SETTING UP YOUR WORKSTATION

Start Organized to Stay Organized

Keeping a clean workstation where items are labeled and in their proper place can save you so much time and prevent many headaches. Even if you think you don't have that much, getting organized early on will help you keep good habits as your business—and, inevitably, your paint stash—grows.

Try to keep the following in designated spaces:

CHALK FINISH PAINT

Keep a few neutral colors on hand. These tend to sell quickly. I like to keep a bright white, a beige or off-white, a light pastel blue or green, and a few shades of gray. When going dark, I think navy and charcoal colors sell well.

SEALANTS

I recommend keeping clear wax, dark wax, white wax, polyacrylic, and polyurethane on hand.

RETIQUE IT®

Keep a few of shades of Retique It® liquid wood on hand. I like to have Bleached Wood, Light Wood, and Dark Wood. You'll also want to keep a few popular stains. My go-to colors are Kona, Ebony, and Weathered Gray.

⋯BRUSHES⋯

Keep three mason jars containing the following types of brushes. One contains nylon/polyester paintbrushes. The second contains cheap chip brushes you don't mind throwing away. The third contains 1.5 to 2" wax brushes (mainly used for waxing and sometimes for chalk finish paint)

When I first started, all I had was the paint and wax and started from there. Your supplies and workstation will evolve and grow over time.

⋯EXTRAS⋯

- Several foam sanding sponges with varying grit levels – fine, medium and coarse
- Disposable paper and/or plastic cups
- Graining tool
- Screwdriver set
- Scissors
- Painter's tape
- A couple drop cloths
- Mineral spirits
- Denatured alcohol
- Clean and lint-free cloth (old socks or cut up t-shirts work well)

⋯NOTE⋯

Don't be overwhelmed if you don't have all these things ALL the time. Each project will remind you when you're running low on something, and you can always replenish your supply as needed. You will quickly learn what products you like best and be able to gauge how much you need for future projects.

MICHELE CORWIN

CHAPTER SEVEN

ROACHES, SMOKE, & STRANGE CHARACTERS

"Value caution in all your dealings with strangers."

Steven Redhead

Furniture-flipping—oh, how I love thee, let me count the ways...

First and foremost, I love nothing more than meeting new people. I do enjoy people, yet I'm more introverted, and it takes me time to get to know people and trust them. But for some reason, when it comes to something I love or am passionate about (like furniture, decorating, and making money), I find it truly enjoyable to talk to, and share with, strangers. I've made many lifelong friends from buying and selling furniture. James and I have met people from all walks of life—young and old, rich and poor, big families and small families. Plus, you get to meet people at pivotal moments in their journey, as well—they may be empty nesting, newly married, recently from another state and into their new home, etc. Most of the people you encounter will be friendly and in a great mood when you meet them because of the nature of what furniture-flipping is about. I'd say that about 90% of the time, it's awesome. But there will be times when it isn't awesome at all, and that is what I want to share with you, here.

In no way do I want you to feel so afraid or overly cautious after reading this chapter that you stop reading and never even try, for fear of failure or of meeting a weirdo. No, don't stop now. It gets good, but I would be remiss if I didn't add this chapter in. Plus, it's just enjoyable reading, and you may get a chuckle or two out of it. It's funny how some of the most difficult situations in life can later serve as the

> **QUICK TIP**
> If buying from individuals is too scary at first, then stick with getting your used furniture from local thrift stores or donation centers like ReStore® and the Salvation Army®. Check them a few times a week and ask the manager which days are best to come in.

ROACHES, SMOKE, AND STRANGE CHARACTERS

FIVE SAFETY PRECAUTIONS

FOR PURCHASING FURNITURE

ONE
Never go alone. Always bring someone with you when picking up furniture.

TWO
Pay attention to the smell of the home and furniture before buying. You don't want to purchase furniture that has a heavy cigarette/smoke smell or mold growing inside of it.

THREE
Open all drawers and handle the furniture a bit to make sure it has good bones and no major structural issues, like cracks or missing parts.

FOUR
Don't lift furniture that is extremely heavy or beyond your ability to move. It's worth it to get help.

FIVE
Check for signs or evidence of bugs, especially roaches. Do not buy anything that has been previously infested with roaches. It's a no-no, which I will go into more detail about in this chapter.

most entertaining and most treasured stories to share with others.

I truly believe that more caution must be taken when purchasing furniture, than compared to selling it. You must be cautious about items for sale that seem too good to be true. It's of the u®ost importance that you trust your instincts when dealing with people. And if you have a funny feeling about meeting someone or going to their home or storage building, then move on and politely pass. There will always be another deal out there to jump on, one that you feel more comfortable with.

NEVER GO ALONE

Let me just start by saying that, in the beginning, buying and selling furniture went against my very nature. I'm an extremely cautious person—so much so that I even admit it can be a little ridiculous. James rolls his eyes a lot about my phobias, but he is a trooper. Just to name a couple: I won't go to the Grand Canyon with the kids, for fear of them falling off the edge, and I get scared taking my kids to the zoo because I'm afraid one of the wild animals will get loose and eat us. Yes, I'm that person. At first, I treat everyone I deal with as a potential serial killer or scammer. I'm a little insane that way, but I share all of this because I know I'm not alone. I don't want any of you to keep your fears from allowing you to find success. I know we've all read about people who have been scammed, hurt, or even killed by someone they met on certain online selling sites. There are a few big ways to prevent this from happening. Never go alone to pick up furniture—only go to locations you feel safe about. It's good to be friendly, ask some questions, and get a good feel for the type of person you're dealing with before you plan to meet up in person.

There have been times when the furniture pick-up address took us to a rural home in the middle of nowhere, and we chose to back out of the deal because it was too shady or didn't feel right. Always remember, it's better to be on the safe side and pick up furniture from neighborhoods and houses that are close together. There may be exceptions, but please use caution if the seller lives in the country, where there doesn't seem to be a living soul for miles and refuses to meet anywhere more public. I advise you to stay in areas that have a lot of people nearby.

I never ever pick up furniture without bringing someone with me. James usually picks it up with me, or he goes with a friend or family member; neither of us ever goes alone. And we only carry the amount of cash required for the purchase, and never more. If it's a very large cash purchase (like over $500), then we request to pay by credit card through one of the many avenues that are available. Carrying around several thousand dollars in cash is just not a good idea. I'm sure you can use your imagination as to why.

REMEMBER THIS PIECE? WHILE IT HAD GOOD BONES IT HAD A A LESS-THAN-DESIRABLE SMELL. IT'S IMPORTANT TO GIVE A PIECE A GOOD CLEANING AND INSPECTION AS SOON AS YOU GET IT HOME.

MICHELE CORWIN

PAY ATTENTION TO THE SMELL

Smell is a big deal to some people. I have a good sniffer, and unfortunately, smell can cause me a lot of grief. There are some people who don't notice strong odors, so this isn't an issue for them, but these days, with the increase in allergies, sensitive noses, and mothers who are cautious with their choice of furniture around small children, it has become an issue. Many of your buyers will ask if your furniture has ever been in a smoker's home or if it has mold. You will want to be able to answer, "No," to these questions and be able to say it honestly.

It's good to ask people about the smoke issue first, before driving a long way to pick up a piece of furniture. Sometimes, even if you ask, you'll realize the seller lied when you get to the location and immediately smell smoke or mold (mold often shows up in black speckling, as well). This is when you should back out and be honest. Say you are sensitive to the smell of smoke or mold. Just be polite and move on. This can happen quite often. Question before you drive; and when you get there, use your nose and your instinct before you buy. Even if you can live with the sometimes pleasantly musty smell of antiques, a potential client might not be able to do so.

There are times when a piece is so amazing that you just can't pass it up, regardless of the smell. If the issue is just smoke, then you can rub the piece down with baking soda and a vinegar-based, mild multipurpose cleaner and then let it dry. After that, you'll want to shellac the piece to seal in the smell, and then you're ready to paint. It can be a lot of extra work, and most of the time, it's not worth the effort, unless the piece is so fabulous that you can't pass it up.

> **QUICK TIP**
>
> Investigate a piece of furniture like you are Sherlock Holmes. Study it and use all of your senses, except for taste (now, that would be weird). Smell it, look closely, move it around, and listen for strange squeaks or crackling sounds.

MAKE SURE IT HAS GOOD "BONES"

It is critical that the piece of furniture you have your sights set on is structurally sound. I still clearly remember the time James picked up a gorgeous French provincial dresser for a killer deal, but when he got it home, I quickly discovered that it smelled like smoke and was coming apart. I probably ended up putting in an extra ten to twelve hours—aside from painting—just to get that thing in shape for resale. I had to use a lot of wood glue and creativity. It really wasn't worth it, in my opinion, but it was a good lesson for us.

It's also important to carefully check dining room chairs before you purchase them—sit in all of them, check their sturdiness, and make sure none of them are missing spindles, are cracked, or have tears in the cane work. All of these things can be repaired, but they need to be pointed out and considered before your price is agreed upon.

The more structurally sound a piece is, the less work involved in the long run. Look for solid materials and check the joints. If you need to make repairs, make sure you account for that in the price. Keep track of your hours. Remember that time = money!

I GOT A GREAT DEAL ON THESE BECAUSE ONE CHAIR NEEDED SOME REPAIRS. RATHER THAN FIX IT, I SAVED TIME AND ONLY USED SIX CHAIRS TO MAKE IT EVEN.

MICHELE CORWIN

DON'T LIFT FURNITURE THAT IS TOO HEAVY

Heavy furniture can kill you, put you in the hospital, or leave you bedridden for weeks because of back injuries. Always make sure you bring enough people to help lift furniture. Remember, there are companies you can pay to do the heavy lifting and delivery for you. Please don't feel like you need to be a superhero like James and I did.

There was one occasion when we met one of the sweetest, most eccentric women I think I've ever known, and she wanted us to help her move two extremely heavy dressers up and down a very steep, old-fashioned staircase. She wanted to buy a dresser from us for her elderly mother, so we thought we'd be gracious enough to help do the heavy lifting. Now, just let me say that while it's good to be charitable, if I had a do-over, I'm not sure I would. We had one of those moments, midway down the stairs, where James and I actually saw our lives flash before our eyes.

I remember praying midway through and asking God to help me. Luckily, at that very moment, the woman's stout daughter saved the day by lifting the dresser higher, and we miraculously managed to get to the bottom level safely. "Never again," I said. I was definitely in fight-or-flight mode. I truly thought I would be on the news for being crushed by a Thomasville® dresser. Well, at least I would have been taken out by a high-quality piece of furniture while doing a good deed (Ha!). Seriously, though, some of that higher-quality furniture can be a beast to lift. Do the "heavy lifting" symbolically. Do not do the heavy lifting literally. It's worth it to get professionals to help... It may save your life.

> **QUICK TIP**
>
> If you don't enjoy heavy lifting, stick with lighter pieces or do an internet search for furniture movers in your area. Find a company you like and bake the expense into your sale price.

CHECK FOR ROACHES AND BUGS

Nobody wants to buy furniture infested with bugs... period.

I still remember the time James proudly came home with a beautiful oak dining room table for me to paint and resell. We had just moved into a brand-new home at the time, and luckily, we were redoing the furniture out in our garage. It was autumn, and the temperature was pleasant enough for us to be outdoors. I quickly began to spray and wipe the table down with a vinegar-based cleaner. When we flipped the table over, I suddenly noticed the remnants of dead roaches hanging underneath. I quickly felt myself go into panic mode, realizing this table may have roaches. I asked James about it, and he proceeded to tell me that the guy who sold him the table was clearing out his rental house. The previous tenants had skipped town and left a bunch of old furniture behind, so he was selling it. We purchased the table for around $80, which we thought was a good deal. Little did we know what was lurking.

As I was spraying and cleaning, James said it looked like the guy must have sprayed roach killer and that I didn't have anything to worry about, since they were all dead. Hey, what did I know about bugs? I thought that was that, and we were good to move forward with the flip. So, I proceeded to clean, and then I pulled the table apart to put in the leaf—that was the moment it turned into a scene from an Alfred Hitchcock movie. It looked like forty or fifty of the creepy crawlers were wiggling out of the base of this old oak table. I screamed and began to do something that resembled a tribal dance. James stayed pretty calm, but I yelled for him to carry it out to the road as

MICHELE CORWIN

fast as he could, for fear of infesting our new house.

Once the table was about fifty feet away, I read up on roaches and found out they can lay eggs inside a table, or in any piece of furniture for that matter, that will continue to hatch after several days. Apparently, roaches like kitchen tables because crumbs and food debris get stuck inside the cracks and crevices. Anyhow, there was no way I was going to sell this roach-infested table to anyone. That felt wrong! So, we did the next logical thing. We posted the table on Craigslist as a "Curb Alert," Basically, we just wanted someone to take it away; we didn't mind giving it away for free if it meant keeping our van and house safe from infestation.

Now, keep in mind that, on this listing, we said, in bold, that the table had roaches. We were completely honest. I'd never forgive myself if I would have misrepresented the information and knowingly given a family roaches. James and I didn't think anyone would pick up the table. We were concerned it would sit on our curb for days. Shockingly, within the first hour, we had over twenty people contact us about wanting the table. It got snatched up within thirty minutes. We even made sure the family who picked it up knew it was infested, but they didn't care. As the saying goes, "One man's trash is another man's treasure."

Despite the stories above, most of our furniture transactions have gone well. People tend to be honest. If you treat them well, they will treat you well. However, there is nothing wrong with using a little care when you flip furniture, insofar as using your basic common sense. This is the bottom-line theme of this chapter.

ROACHES, SMOKE, AND STRANGE CHARACTERS

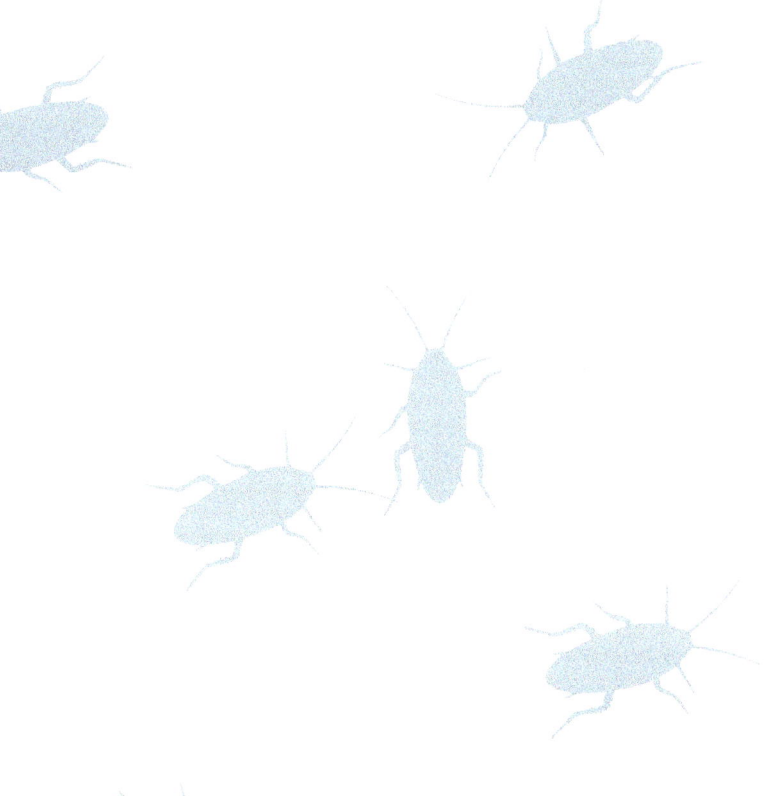

QUICK TIP

Look out for bedbugs, roaches, and spider eggs! Bedbugs like to hide in wood and in the crevices of bedroom furniture. If you do run into bedbugs, walk away from the piece immidiately and treat your clothing and vehicle! I promise no piece is worth bringing bedbugs home!

MICHELE CORWIN

CHAPTER EIGHT

SELLING SITES & PRICING

> "The salesman knows nothing of what he is selling save that he is charging a great deal too much for it."
>
> Oscar Wilde

I still get a good chuckle when I surf the numerous selling sites out there for selling furniture and, well, pretty much everything else—everything from belly button lint to a human hamster wheel. You can't make this stuff up, folks! Seriously, though, I'm telling you all of this so you won't talk yourself out of selling furniture because it sounds too complicated or out of your reach. Believe me, it's as easy as using social media. Almost everyone knows what hashtags and tweets are these days. Am I right? If you're a newbie to this, you're in luck! This is the perfect time to start a furniture-flipping business.

Technology is on your side, my friend. All you need is a smartphone and/or a computer, along with the knowledge of how to take a picture (it's just like taking a good selfie). I love that I can pretty much use my smartphone to run my whole business. I can find my next piece of furniture to flip, communicate with customers, take pictures, and even post them along with a simple description. The awesome part is that these selling apps make your business a cinch.

I thought flipping furniture was pretty easy when I first started about five years ago, but now, it's even easier. It's quite exciting, seeing how things have evolved since the days of just yard sales and flea markets, when platforms like Craigslist and eBay were just beginning. I sort of feel like a dinosaur because I got into this business when it was all about Craigslist. Now, I love Facebook Marketplace, OfferUp, and occasionally, Letgo. These platforms all notify you about good buys (set to your specifications), let you rate the people you're dealing with, and even view sellers through their social media profiles (see my chapter about shady characters). It's also super convenient how all of your communications are organized under each item. Juggling and selling multiple items couldn't be easier.

SELLING AND DELIVERY APPS

From my experience, I like selling on Facebook Marketplace, but I also see the value of OfferUp. In our area, things don't get snatched up as quickly on OfferUp, which makes it great for buying. Each app has a slightly different feel. I'm more comfortable with Marketplace because I'm on Facebook every day anyway, and it was simple to set up through my Facebook account.

I'm going to list some other sites for selling your furniture, but from my experience, and in my area, I like Craigslist, Facebook Marketplace, OfferUp, and Letgo the best. That doesn't mean you won't prefer

> **QUICK TIP**
>
> Start by selling locally and really work to develop your craft and style. As you get more established, consider selling outside of your local area. Some of the high-end selling sites (like Chairish) offer a white-glove delivery service. Remember to consider delivery when pricing your piece.

some of the other apps. It's all a matter of preference and what is popular in your neck of the woods. I encourage you to try them all out if you're feeling adventurous. Just keep in mind, I've shared the selling sites on which I've personally had the most success because I found them to be, quite frankly, easy enough for a child to use.

Check out these other sites for selling furniture online—see the following, listed in no special order, as of 2019 (keep in mind, the popularity of these may change):

SELLING SITES

- eBay
- OfferUp
- Etsy
- AptDeco
- Chairish
- Shopify
- Geebo
- Kijiji (Canada)
- LetGo
- Amazon

Selling apps will come and go. Stay current and do your research to keep up with trends.

QUICK TIP

Stick with local sites like Marketplace, Offerup, Craigslist, and Letgo for buying if you want to avoid long-distance shipping charges. You can also buy from your local thrift store, but make sure you have a way to transport your purchases!

DELIVERY OPTIONS

There are also several companies with apps you can use to do your furniture delivery for you. Two that come to mind are GoShare and uShip. There are several other local ones out there, though, and the delivery market is always evolving. But just know that you're not alone if you're doing this furniture-flipping business on your own. You don't have to do any of the heavy lifting if you don't want to. Delivery services can make things super easy for you if you don't have a truck and/or van to haul the furniture in. They will also save your back.

Customers love it when you offer them the option of delivery. Just make sure to factor in the delivery cost when selling to your buyers. It's good to get a free estimate first, so you know what you're dealing with, in terms of cost. Sometimes, this can make the price of your piece go up considerably.

You're probably a little overwhelmed with anticipation after reading about delivery options and the selling-app list, but I want you to realize that you'll probably find only one or two sites on the list that you'll decide to use on a regular basis. One thing to note is that pricing can drastically vary from site to site. Some of the sites, like Marketplace on Facebook will even give you a suggested range of pricing for your specific item. I've found, the more artsy sites, like Etsy, boast a much higher price tag (because you're selling a work of art) and may take much longer to bring in sales. The optimal length of time that you should wait for an item to sell is relative to what kind of profit you're going for, as well as the popularity of a particular item in your city.

If you happen to live in a city with a low population that doesn't seem to sell much furniture, then I'd invite you to consider selling on eBay, Etsy, or even Amazon Handmade (for artisans). The shipping can seem tricky, but currently, you can use Uship. The Uship website has detailed instructions that describe how to properly ship larger furniture items. Just make sure you get a good estimate for the cost, and bake that into the price so you can make a good profit. You can ask for more money on these sites; using a high-end site is like selling a custom piece in a boutique.

If all of that seems overwhelming, then don't give up on trying the more local selling sites. If you live in a small town, your items may take longer to sell, but you'll most likely gain some really good contract work. Customers in small towns (or any town) can get excited when they find someone who will paint furniture for them and give it a high-end, custom look. Every market is a little different, so it may take a month or two to get into the groove of the market. Also, keep in mind that, from Thanksgiving to mid-February, sales can be a little on the slow side, in some regions, but the rest of the year will make up for it.

The slow time is good for you to get caught up on all of your projects and prepare for the busy season ahead. Pricing can seem tricky, but it's super easy.

As I've stated in previous chapters, I started out selling items too cheaply, therefore undervaluing my labor. This caused me to have to do double the work, for basically the same amount of money, but I quickly found out that raising the prices on my furniture and time meant I could make a lot more profit for a lot less work, and in the same amount of time. Yes, you read that right—the same amount of time. This just requires a little more patience. Let's look at an example:

On June 1st, you list a dining room set for $650, and you end up selling it by June 11th for $580. So, it took a week and a half to sell. The cost of refinishing, in this set was a total of $220. Your profit would be $360. You spent a total of eight hours driving to pick up the set, painting the wood, and reupholstering the seat cushions. This means that you averaged about $45 an hour for your work—not bad, I'd say.

Now, let's consider what it would mean if you had chosen to hold on to the dining room set a bit longer and had waited another week to receive the full asking price of $650. If you had the patience to wait, it would mean that your profit would be $430, and you would have averaged a little over $53 an hour.

You see what a difference a little patience can make.

As my business became more profitable, I could allow for more time to relax. It's funny, and a little sad, when I consider the time I spent my first week compared to when I became more experienced. Now, I can make the same amount of money selling two higher-priced items in one month than I can selling twenty lower-priced items, which is what I did when I first started. Oh, and the two higher-priced items only required about ten hours of work, compared to a hefty seventy to eighty hours to sell the twenty lower-priced items. The trade-off seems like a no-brainer, but I think my early workload was worth it for the education. I learned so much through the experience and I gained future customers, which made those extra hours well worth it.

MICHELE CORWIN

EIGHT TIPS

For Setting a Good Price

ONE

Check out similar items and see what they're going for. Stay within this range or come up with a clear reason for setting higher prices.

TWO

Consider what the item would cost if it were brand-new. If buying brand-new is cheaper, virtually everyone would choose to buy new.

THREE

If you get more than five people interested within the first hour of listing, you've priced the item too low, and you're practically giving it away. My tip is to edit your listing and go up in price. Unfortunately, you cannot go up in price for the people who express interest in the item at the lower price.

FOUR

It's always better to start out a little high and drop the price if you don't get any bites within the first day or two.

...FIVE...

Keep your word on pricing, once you've committed to a price with a buyer—even if it means giving up on a later offer that is a little higher. From experience, I believe, in this case, you reap what you sow.

...SIX...

Consider renewing or boosting your listing to the top before lowering the price.

...SEVEN...

Remember, patiently waiting for a higher price means you'll end up doing less work for the same amount of money.

...EIGHT...

Never forget, you're in this for a profit. Keep track of your costs and consider the time you've put into your piece of furniture. Don't forget to take into consideration the miles driven, as well.

CHAPTER NINE

HAGGLING

"No one should drive a hard bargain with an artist."

Ludwig van Beethoven

I'm sure many of you are beginning this chapter thinking that you hate haggling over a price. You may have been taught that it's rude not to offer the asking price. Visions of shady used-car salesmen, wearing cheap suits and smoking cigars come to mind. Sorry, I got a little carried away.

Anyhow, all kidding aside... I want you to take all of those preconceived notions and throw them out the window. I'm going to train you how to be a ninja negotiator. It's simple and quite fun. It is probably the most integral part of making a profit—it's even more important than learning painting techniques.

There are two types of furniture-flipping. The first type is simply buying low and selling high. The second is to buy low, repair, paint, and sell for a much higher price because the piece has now become a work of art. Obviously, the latter requires more time and effort but usually gives you a much higher profit. I say "usually" because I can recall there were times when this had not been true. Sometimes no real work had to be done to a piece, except a little cleanup and staging with pictures in order to resell for a profit. Either way, you'll quickly discover that haggling or negotiating is a necessary skill for buying, as well as selling.

Please don't be intimidated or overwhelmed by my last statement. You can still make money if you don't know how to haggle properly; you just won't make as much as you could. I want you to think of haggling as your favorite game, which you get to play whenever you feel like it through your computer. It's fun and addictive. You can be extremely polite, even when people lowball you or you feel like lowballing someone. There is skill involved in making offers, being kind and considerate, and still getting an awesome deal! Just know that people can get offended easily, and sometimes the slightest difference in wording can change your tone significantly. The following is an example: You see a dining room table for sale for $180. You want to flip it for $280. That sale would give you a profit of under $100 dollars when you factor in driving time for pickup, as well as any repairs, staining, or repainting you'll need to do. So, the key is to try to get them down on their price.

Your first inclination might be to say, "I like your table. Will you take $100?" But I've found a better way of wording it is to say, "I love your table. It's just what I'm looking for, but I can only pay $100. Please let me know ASAP, so I can pick it up this afternoon or in the morning." You want to convey that you have limited funds but you can take the item off their hands quickly. This is generally a plus for the seller.

Now, I'd like to give you some advice that works on the other end of the deal. You're the one selling the table now. You've spent six hours total, when you combine driving time and your hours repainting the piece, and a potential buyer says that all they can pay you is $100 for the $300 table you're offering. Your first impulse may be to get offended that they don't see the value in your work, but they're just testing the waters. You respond by saying that you can do $280, if they come by to pick it up within the next twenty-four hours. Try to convey how popular the style is and that you've received a lot of interest in the piece.

> **··QUICK TIP··**
> Don't be afraid to be a ninja negotiator when buying and selling. If it's going to add to your time, make note of that and stay adamant about the money you are willing to spend or receive, in order to make a reasonable profit.

The buyer may say they can pay more, or they may not. You'll know how far you're willing to drop the asking price. Just make sure that you get paid for all of your hard work and that you're making a decent profit. Think about all of the expenses involved, as well as your time. It's important! Your time is valuable, and as you develop your painting and flipping skills, you're also growing as an artisan. You'll want to stay in touch with what's popular—buy a couple of decorating magazines every month to maintain an evolving awareness of your new business (search current decorating trends).

When I first started flipping furniture, I truly had no clue what I was doing. I would keep the furniture cheaply priced so that it would sell within a day. I later learned that I was running myself ragged. It's better to bump up the price a bit, be patient, and hold out a week or two so you can be properly compensated for the time, money, and effort you've invested into each piece.

There is so much you'll learn about haggling from trial and error. It's like any game—the more you play, the better you'll get at it. Still, I want to save you some of the grief I had to go through, so I've written out some basic rules to get you started. I had to go to the school of hard knocks when it came to furniture-flipping, but the lessons have forever been seared into my brain.

RULES FOR SELLING FURNITURE

ONE

The Golden Rule: Never sell a piece of furniture you wouldn't want to own if you were in the market. It's important that you believe you're doing right by your customer.

TWO

Be honest and trustworthy. It's the right thing to do. People will come back to you for furniture and contract work in the future if you have a good reputation and they know they can trust you. Contract work is a potential expansion of your initial flipping work. When you develop a good reputation, people may want to hire you to fix or refinish their furniture. They may even commission you to find specific pieces for them. You can expand a successful flipping business. You can also gain a fair degree of personal satisfaction and profit from just continuing with flipping.

THREE

Set a fair price and then list your furniture piece(s) for slightly above that price, allowing room for negotiation. Everyone wants to feel like they're getting a deal. Make sure you get the profit you planned on.

RULES FOR PURCHASING FURNITURE

ONE

It never hurts to ask. If you see a beautiful piece of furniture, you can always offer a price much lower than the asking price. Remember, it really doesn't hurt to ask. Just be respectful and say that you're only able to offer a certain amount. If they say no, then kindly thank them for their consideration and tell them to contact you if they change their mind.

TWO

Don't haggle yourself out of a good deal.
Enough said!

THREE

Do your research and know the value of the piece you're looking at. This will develop over time.

FOUR

Consider the distance you'll have to drive as part of the cost of the piece.

FIVE

Ask questions about the piece prior to agreeing on a price. Ask if the furniture has been in a smoker's home, if it's structurally sound, and if there is anything special you should know about the piece. Once you decide on a price over social media apps or email, don't ever allow the seller to raise the price, once you arrive for pickup. If they do, walk away from the deal. This behavior shows that they are not trustworthy!

Number five in the purchasing rules is so critical; it's where I learned some of my most painful lessons. Ask the right questions prior to driving all the way over to someone's storage unit or house to pick up the furniture. You'll save yourself a lot of trouble. Also, trust your instincts. If the person sounds shady or unreliable, don't deal with them. I touched on this in chapter seven. Needless to say, there were several times we drove thirty to forty-five minutes out of our way and came back empty-handed because we didn't ask the right questions first.

The buying and selling rules can be summed up in two words: "honesty" and "integrity." But never forget that you still have the goal of making a profit. If you master the purchasing rules, it will be become easier to follow the three selling rules. It's important to study these rules and keep them in mind when communicating with your customers and other sellers. Don't get too stressed out about them though. I know they can seem overwhelming. Just remember that every game, no matter how much fun, must have some solid rules. You can do this. You'll make some mistakes along the way, but it's all okay, though, because you're learning, and that's a good thing.

CHAPTER TEN

MORE THAN A HOBBY

> "The hardest thing in the world to understand is the income tax."
>
> *Albert Einstein*

That's right, folks—taxes can get complicated. In fact, taxes can get so tricky and stressful that most of us try to push the process to the back of our minds each year until just before April 15th. Unfortunately, for about ten years, I didn't have the luxury of forgetting about taxes because I was an accountant at a small CPA firm. That's right, creative me was stuck in an accounting office for that long. I had taxes on the brain for a while, and they were my life for many years. I used to balance the books and do tax returns for several corporations, all the while dreaming of owning my own successful business one day.

Although those ten years were difficult, I'm grateful for my lifelong friends from the office and for what I learned. So, this is my bit of advice for you. I can sum it all up in one sentence worthy of bold typeface:

GET YOURSELF A CPA ASAP!

If you're reading this book and you've already made some profit selling furniture, then most likely, you need to consider what you're doing as a "business." Once furniture-flipping goes from being a hobby to a business, you'll want to get a CPA. "But how do I know if it's a business or a hobby?" you may ask.

QUICK TIP

Talk to other local business owners in your area and ask questions. Most people will be more than happy to share information about laws in your area and advice on how they got started. This is also a great way to start networking.

Here is what the IRS says on the subject (per IRS publication 535, Business Expenses):

> In general, taxpayers may deduct ordinary and necessary expenses for conducting a trade or business. An ordinary expense is an expense that is common and accepted in the taxpayer's trade or business. A necessary expense is one that is appropriate for the business. Generally, an activity qualifies as a business if it is carried on with the reasonable expectation of earning a profit.
>
> In order to make this determination, taxpayers should consider the following factors:
>
> - Does the time and effort put into the activity indicate an intention to make a profit?
> - Does the taxpayer depend on income from the activity?
> - If there are losses, are they due to circumstances beyond the taxpayer's control or did they occur in the start-up phase of the business?
> - Has the taxpayer changed methods of operation to improve profitability?
> - Does the taxpayer or his/her advisors have the knowledge needed to carry on the activity as a successful business?
> - Has the taxpayer made a profit in similar activities in the past?
> - Does the activity make a profit in some years?
> - Can the taxpayer expect to make a profit in the future from the appreciation of assets used in the activity?

Regardless of the conclusion you come to after reading the IRS information, I implore you to keep good records and get a CPA (Certified Public Accountant). Even if you're dealing in cash, you'll need to keep track of what you're purchasing and what you're selling.

An easy way of doing this is to keep a three-ringed binder filled with before-and-after pictures of the items you've bought and sold (this doubles as a portfolio, which can impress clients and allow you to see how you've evolved as an artist). You can also keep a record on your computer of the before-and-after shots. With the "before" picture, you'll want to attach your purchase price (plus, include a separate note with any receipts for supplies you purchased for the flip, especially if you're dealing in cash). With the "after" picture, you'll want to write down the price you sold the piece of furniture for. You'll want to keep track of your mileage and gas receipts as well. There are several phone apps that can help you keep track of business mileage. Your CPA will thank you because you can email your mileage reports to them from your phone. It doesn't get any easier than this, folks.

At first, your business will be a sole proprietorship. Later, your CPA can help you decide if it would be advantageous for you to change the entity type to something like an LLC or a corporation.

Don't forget to look at local business laws and regulations for your area. It may not be a problem if you just flip an occasional piece, but it could become an issue if you start doing this full-time. Look up your local government website. They will likely have a page for small businesses or something similar.

> **QUICK TIP**
>
> Trello (a project organization tool) is a great way to organize your pictures of before and afters and attach your expenses, mileage, and selling prices. It will also help you organize your time and have great reference pictures on hand.

GETTING ORGANIZED

MY REASONS FOR GETTING A CPA

ONE
It will save you time and money in the long run. Monthly bookkeeping and tax preparation fees from a CPA are probably cheaper than if you tried to do it all on your own or hired an employee to do it for you full time.

TWO
CPAs can help you get set up for sales taxes, as well as payroll taxes, if you choose to hire employees in the future. You'll want to apply for an EIN (Employer Identification Number) and acquire a sales tax number, which you'll need to apply for during your first month of sales, if applicable for your state.

THREE
Tax laws are constantly changing. I can't keep up with all of the new laws anymore. That is why I have a CPA.

FOUR
CPAs can advise you about how to be more profitable as a business and keep you from missing out on big write-offs.

FIVE
A CPA can advise you about switching from a sole proprietorship to a limited liability company or corporation when the time comes.

COMING UP WITH A BUSINESS NAME

In the beginning, you don't have to come up with a name for your business, but eventually, it will be a good idea to name it something you'll be proud of, something that represents you and your style.

A lot of people get caught up trying to figure out a business name before they even start flipping their first piece of furniture. This is what I did. I got caught up in figuring out a name for my business, and I sort of got stuck in my own head, if you will. When I look back, it seems a little silly that I spent so much time considering possible name options, but it made it feel more real, and it got my creative juices flowing. This is all important in building your passion and your dream. Anything you can do to help yourself get excited and inspired about your business is a good thing. For me, the name also helped when setting up my social media accounts, which showcased my business and all of my furniture transformations. Just remember to keep your business name original and classy. It should represent something that inspires you.

The key to all of this is to get a vision and stay inspired. After reading this chapter, I hope you have a clearer picture of all that this venture entails when it comes to business and financial planning. It's truly as simple as coming up with a business name while you paint your first piece of furniture, and then contacting a CPA after you make your first few sales. I want you to see that you don't have to have any business background, even though I did. This process is simple enough for almost anyone, and it's possible to have more time to enjoy working at your new business rather than spending all your time worrying about finances. Don't forget, the whole point of this is to gain financial freedom and have more quality time to hang out with your family and friends, doing what you love most.

> **QUICK TIP**
> As soon as you pick your business name, you should create business pages on social media under the new name. Don't be afraid to promote it on your personal pages as well!

CHAPTER ELEVEN

THE SKY IS NOT THE LIMIT

> "The sky is not the limit. Your mind is."
>
> *Marilyn Monroe*

If you haven't gotten your feet wet and tried something outside of your comfort zone in a while, then you're probably a procrastinator like I once was.

Do you study every idea to death, but never do anything? Sound familiar?

If so, then I'd like to introduce you to a concept that has the ability to make you a doer and not just a dreamer.

There is this fantastic, and oh-so-simple, Japanese technique I learned called Kaizen.

Kaizen is basically the "one-minute rule." What I mean by "one minute" is that you must spend at least one minute each day doing something that will move you in the direction of your goal.

This must become a routine and be done around the same time every day.

You're probably thinking that "one minute" sounds ridiculous, but it's truly not. Here's why: Most people talk themselves out of following their dreams because they think it involves too much time and effort that may ultimately result in failure. Kaizen eliminates this

> **QUICK TIP**
> Make a fresh list of your dreams every week. After that, list out some goals you can conquer this week in order to move toward these dreams. Then, practice the "one-minute" rule of kaizen to get yourself going.

issue completely by tricking your brain into letting you work. Your mind classifies spending one minute doing anything as easy! You see... even if you consider yourself a lazy human being, this technique will still work for you.

The most difficult part of achieving anything is deciding to do it. I believe that most of us suffer from what I call "inertia disorder."

This is basically the condition where you have difficulty getting motivated and feeling driven. In truth, you don't need to get that excited about one minute of work.

Here's what's going to happen, though—you're going to get started, and one minute will go by, and you'll decide to give it more time because you've already fought the hardest battle—the battle of the mind! This is the battle that keeps you from starting and finishing anything.

Every time you conquer this battle, you will create grooves in your brain that will change your inner monologue and self-image forever. You will be creating new habits and new ways of thinking. With the help of Kaizen, and utilizing some of these tips, you will far exceed your dreams of making money, enjoying your work, and finding success!

You can take this business to whatever level you want. You can make it full-time or part-time. You can make it a six- or even seven-figure-income business. I'm going to give you some examples of what an average day might look like with different scenarios, along with potential income levels you may reach in your business.

---

*The principal of Kaizen is described by Masaaki Imai in his 1986 book, *Kaizen: The Key to Japan's Competitive Success*.

PART-TIME OPTION

7:00 a.m. – Wake up and get ready for the day.

8:00 a.m. – Run some errands, take kids to school.

9:00 a.m. – Enjoy you morning coffee/breakfast while responding to emails/messages regarding offers on current furniture listings you've posted.

9:30 a.m. – Look through furniture listings. Search for potential great deals in your area and make some offers.

10:00 a.m. – Start your current project: get painting/staining. Make sure to take before-and-after pictures for your portfolio.

1:15 p.m. – Eat lunch and allow your project to dry.

2:00 p.m. – You're done… You've achieved a lot! Get prepped for the next day's work. Enjoy the rest of your day with friends and family.

*Keep an eye out for messages from potential buyers and sellers throughout the day; some cell phone apps will alert you when a new listing comes up, according to the criteria you have set. This is how you can get the best deals and jump on listings while they're hot!

(With the part-time method, you can potentially net anywhere from $1,000 to $4,000 per month, and you only need to invest about twenty to thirty hours of work a week. Adding an employee or two can increase your income without adding more hours for you).

> **QUICK TIP**
>
> Planning your day is the foundation for organization and success. Don't forget to plan time for fun and relaxation. Set a time to turn off your cell phone, notifications, and computer if you want to keep your sanity.

FULL-TIME OPTION

6:00 a.m. – Shower and get ready for the day.

7:30 a.m. – Have coffee/breakfast and greet your employees.

8:00 a.m. – Set a plan for what needs to be picked up, delivered, and painted/stained/reupholstered for the day.

8:30 a.m. – Carry out the plan for the day.

12:00 p.m. – Lunch.

1:00 p.m. – Carry out the plan for the rest of the day.

5:00 p.m. – You're finished! You and your employees have finished several pieces of furniture and listed them for sale. You've also shown some pieces during the day to buyers and managed to sell a few items while your employees were busy at work.

With the "full-time option," you have the potential to net anywhere from $4,000 to $20,000-plus per month, especially if you hire a couple employees and do contract work (painting/staining cabinets, accent walls, and flooring).

You may also decide that your business has grown large enough to open up your own shop. This will allow for other revenue streams, like holding in-store training workshops, teaching people how to paint, selling painting products, and opening up other stores in your region.

Your mind is literally the limit here

Another option is consulting or coaching other people online who want to learn about flipping furniture. You can start your own community on social media and advertise a small amount per day to gain members and invite them to join your signature system.

You can also create classes in modules online and sell your online training program. There are several options for creating and selling your online teaching modules—this is always evolving.

This may all sound overwhelming to a person who is new to flipping furniture, but I want you to know that you can truly make this process your own. There are so many directions in which you can take this—so many methods of earning income.

All you need to do is make the decision to move forward with your intentions. That one small step each day is all it takes.

Remember the kaizen rule and don't get too overwhelmed.

Think about all I've shared about my story... all the way back to my humble beginning and the $10 table.

You must start somewhere, and then just keep on trucking!

You've heard it before, but Rome wasn't built in a day.

It will take you about a month to feel like you're getting into the swing of things, and then you'll feel comfortable enough to let your dream grow a little bigger (remember the "snowball effect"). It will only take a few sales to spark your excitement and give you even greater inspiration for your business.

Learn to listen to the inspirational thoughts that

come to you throughout the day—these are little gifts to help guide you along, to help you achieve your dreams. Don't discredit any inspiration that comes to you, no matter how crazy it seems.

Inspiration will often come in a flash. I would like to say:

Wait...For...It. Inspiration usually comes when you're not even thinking about it.

While it can come when you're resting, it usually comes when you're working or "doing," when you're in the groove of things.

That's why the principal of kaizen is so fantastic—it gets you "doing." Even with its simplicity, doing something for just a few minutes each day is the key to unlocking the door to your dreams of success.

One of my most daring yet exciting business endeavors was creating my own product line.

I believe that having a tangible product to sell opened up so many doors. It's where my lifestyle really changed, and I was able to send my kids to private schools, buy nice new vehicles, go on dream vacations, and buy my dream home.

The cool thing is that almost anybody can brand themselves and come up with their own product line these days. But will it be successful? It's not easy—you have to know the right people or spend years doing research. A great product without the right marketing is like a beautiful song that nobody will ever hear.

That's where I come in. I blazed my own trail in brand development and marketing. I've learned that the marketing techniques I was taught years ago have become antiquated. The game has changed. Television, radio, and newspapers are no longer the driving force for gathering a customer base on a small budget these days. Yet, it has never been easier to scale a business.

Many of you may read this chapter and think it's too lofty, and that is okay. You'll know when you've found your place of business bliss. I might argue that true satisfaction comes through continuing to challange yourself, learning new things, and setting new goals.

I've learned, over the years, that the only limitations we truly have are self-imposed. The mind is a wondrous thing, and if we keep it open to new ideas and inspiration, then it won't matter how humble our beginnings were or how hopeless our past felt. Today is the day to flip our living and give ourselves the time to focus on our favorite things and the people we love most.

FREQUENTLY ASKED QUESTIONS

TROUBLE SHOOTING & PAINTING TECHNIQUES

Photo Credit: Sheryl Marlee

PAINTING FURNITURE - THE BASICS

What prep work is required before I begin painting?

Other than ensuring your piece is free of dirt, dust, chipping or grease, there is no extra prep work involved! Simply apply the paint directly to the clean surface.

On what surfaces can I use chalk finish paint?

Wood, metal, glass, plastic, veneer, even fabric! It will adhere to virtually any surface. For fabric, just remember to mix equal parts water and paint. Get a spray bottle filled with water and lightly mist your fabric before applying two to three very light layers of paint. My little tip is to practice on an old throw pillow or pair of jeans a few times, in order to build up your confidence. It's pretty amazing when you realize you can actually paint that beautiful old Victorian chair instead of paying a professional hundreds of dollars to reupholster it.

Do I have to seal chalk finish paint once it's dried?

Yes. Because chalk finish furniture paint is porous, it requires a sealant to protect it from getting stained. We recommend using Retique It ® Furniture Wax, Fiddes Hard Wax Oil, or a polyacrylic (like our Retique It ® Polyacrylic).

QUICK TIP

Never apply polyacrylic over a waxed finish. You can wax over poly with no problem (I do this on all of my tabletops/dresser-tops for extra protection). Just remember, the wax application should be your last step, and you should always do a base of clear wax and buff it out before applying dark wax to light colors. The clear wax can act like an erasing and blending tool (because of the mineral spirits it contains). Clear wax can only erase unwanted or excess dark wax if you have first put a base-layer of clear wax (that's been properly buffed out) over your surface. This is critical to remember if you're dealing with dark wax.

My piece of furniture has wax all over it from a couple of years prior. Can I paint over it? If not, then how do I remove the wax?

I do not recommend painting over a waxed surface. Be sure to remove any wax, grease, or other oil-based substance from the surface before you begin painting. There are many products that can remove wax, but a simple and inexpensive choice is wiping it down with mineral spirits or denatured alcohol. I recommend that waxing is always the last and final step in your project!

I don't see a color offered that I need. What now?

Retique It ® by Renaissance Chalk Finish Paint offers easy online ordering with custom tinting of any major brand! Simply, provide the brand and color name/number, and we will match it. Alternatively, chalk finish paint mixes extremely well! You can combine various colors to get the perfect shade you're looking for!

Is there any odor with chalk finish paint and can I use chalk finish paint inside when I can't open the windows?

Retique It ® Chalk Finish Paint has virtually no odor, and many chalk finish paints out there are low or zero VOCs. It was very important to me that Retique It ® Chalk Finish Paint had zero VOCs.

Is there any special brush I must use to apply chalk finish paint?

No! While I recommend a high-quality (synthetic) brush like our Retique It ® Professional Paint Brush to help minimize brushstrokes (I prefer angled/small handle brushes), you can use whatever brush you'd like, even the natural bristle oval brushes. Please note that the natural bristle oval "Chalk Finish Paint" brushes are for achieving a vintage look, and they will leave lines that give lots of character, especially if you choose to clear- and dark-wax your piece of furniture for that lovely vintage look.

How do I prepare the paint?

In all cases, be sure the top of the paint container is secure, then shake container. Open container and stir the paint thoroughly just prior to application.

MICHELE CORWIN

TECHNIQUES AND APPLICATION

I have an old dresser I'm trying to paint white. I keep getting red and pink bleed-through no matter how many coats of paint I put on. What should I do?

This is common with pieces of furniture that are very old, and it can be extremely frustrating if you've never dealt with it before. The answer to stopping bleed-through is to apply a couple of coats of shellac or polyurethane over the surface and then allow it to dry. After the surface is dry, then apply the paint again. There should be no bleed-through because the shellac/polyurethane creates a barrier. You can also prevent bleed-through by applying a stain-blocking primer.

I messed up and put too much dark wax directly on my light-colored, chalk painted surface. I forgot to do a layer of clear wax first, and now my furniture looks dirty. How can I fix this?

Dampen a clean cloth with mineral spirits and wipe off any unwanted dark wax. Unfortunately, this may remove some paint. You may need to do a touch-up coat of paint after you remove the dark wax. Always remember to apply a layer of clear wax before applying dark wax to any light-colored surface, otherwise it can get too much of a "dirty" look. It's perfectly fine to apply dark wax directly to dark colors, but be aware that you won't be able to remove any excess wax easily, unless you apply a layer of clear wax prior to dark-waxing.

I want to paint a dining room tabletop, but I'm scared it won't be durable enough to eat on daily. What do I seal the paint with?

For extra protection, I recommend sealing your tabletop with polyacrylic, polyurethane, or Fiddes Hard Wax Oil. The Retique It ® Polyacrylic is great for sealing colors that are white, as it is water-based, and it won't yellow them.

I am applying the paint, but it seems too streaky and has too many brushstrokes for my taste. What am I doing wrong?

Make sure you are using a nylon/polyester brush rather than a natural bristle brush. Natural bristle brushes leave brushstrokes. Also, remember to dampen your paintbrush in between brushstrokes to keep things smooth and flowing. You can also lightly sand in between coats for a factory finish.

I've painted the surface several times, but it won't adhere well to certain areas. What should I do?

Make sure you've cleaned the surface properly. You may need to wipe the surface down with denatured alcohol to make sure it's squeaky clean. Dirt, oil, or grease buildup on the surface will repel the paint.

I'm trying to "distress" my piece of furniture, but the paint won't come off. What am I doing wrong?

Make sure all surfaces are the same type of wood and that they've been sealed in the same manner, if you plan on "distressing" the piece by scuffing it up with a sander, later. Some paneling is extremely porous and will absorb the paint more than other surfaces.

How do I get an antique look with chalk finish paint?

For a detailed step-by-step, check out Retique It ® Chalk Finish Paint's tutorial videos—click on the tab called "waxing" for videos on how to get the old, antique look. Use the following website: RetiqueIt.tv

How can I get a weathered look using chalk finish paint?

The weathered wood look is best achieved on oak or wood with a deep grain. Start by watering down the paint in a separate container so that it's smooth and flowing. Use only a dry brush, and very lightly apply one coat in the direction of the woodgrain only. Blot with a clean, dry cloth until you achieve your desired look. It's recommended that paint be sealed after it is thoroughly dry (see directions on clear wax application).

MICHELE CORWIN

I don't like the shabby look. Can I get a clean finish with chalk finish paint?

Yes! If shabby chic is not the look you're going for, simply apply another coat of paint. You can get a clean, smooth finish with our paint! Make sure that, in between strokes, you keep your brush damp to keep things smooth and flowing. I like to keep a plastic cup with water by my side to dip into as needed. This provides a nice uniform look after it dries.

How do I get a smooth-finish/full-coverage look with chalk finish paint

Always make sure your brush is dampened with water in between brushstrokes for a smooth contemporary finish.

Apply paint evenly across the entire piece in one coat, working the brush in the direction of the dgrain.

Leave paint to dry thoroughly. Drying time may take twenty minutes or more—possibly up to a few hours, depending on the humidity.

A second coat may be applied in the same manner, but it can also be applied more heavily, if desired. Allow second coat to dry thoroughly. A third (touch-up) coat is usually not necessary for lighter colors but may be needed on some of the yellows, reds, and greens in our pallet.

How do I achieve the weathered wood look on natural wood surfaces?

This look is best suited to oak or wood with a deep grain. Start by watering down the paint in a separate container so it is smooth and flowing.

Use only a dry brush. Very lightly apply one coat in the direction of the woodgrain only and blot with a clean, dry cloth until you achieve your desired look. I recommend sealing the paint after it is thoroughly dry.

How do I achieve a classic shabby or distressed look?

Follow instructions for a smooth finish/full coverage. Scuff paint from edges and molding with sandpaper as much as needed to achieve the desired level of "distressing." Distressing can be done before or after the wax application.

How do I use wax to seal my painted furniture?

You can seal your piece by applying a thin layer of our clear wax all over the painted area once it has fully dried. A wax brush is best for application, especially when there is intricate molding involved.

Wipe off excess wax using a clean, lint-free cloth, and gently polish the furniture. The degree of sheen will depend on the number of wax layers applied and the intensity of buffing away the excess wax.

Dark wax is optional, and application should be focused on the edges, details, and intricate molding. The clear wax can be used as an eraser to remove any excess dark wax. A glaze is another option and can be made by mixing the clear and dark wax together in a separate container until it becomes liquid. Your glaze can then be applied all over with a brush and polished.

> **QUICK TIP**
>
> If you get stuck and think you've messed up your project, remember that almost everything is fixable. Don't be afraid to contact the makers of the products you use or troubleshoot through furniture-flipping groups and forums. While there are an endless supply of wonderful groups and communities for furniture care and flipping, my "Next Level Flipping - Retique It" group on Facebook is a great place to start! Don't get caught up on mistakes—there is always a next step!

RETIQUE IT ® LIQUID WOOD

What shade of Retique It® liquid wood should I use?

Light Wood is the most versatile of all our wood shades. It gives the greatest depth/contrast, especially when paired with dark stains.
- Works well with any color stain except dark cherry
- Makes a great base coat when using the graining tool
- Dark stains come out as light or dark as you want depending on how long you let it absorb. Follow wood stain directions to see the range of time for absorption.

Dark Wood has deep warm undertones, giving less contrast when used with darker stains.
- Commonly used for the graining coat over light wood
- Light Wood is usually a better choice for dark stains.
- Dark Wood is the best choice for a dark cherry stain.
- Use Dark Wood with dark stains if you don't want as much variation/depth between the stain and the wood.

Golden Pine gives you a beautiful golden undertone and exceptional contrast and depth for darker stains.
- Gray stains are usually not a good choice with Golden Pine.
- Brings out brings out black and brown stains.

Bleached Wood gives you fresh new looks with traditional wood stains.
- Bleached Wood makes it look like you sanded down your piece and soaked the wood in bleach.
- White & gray stains absorb true-to-color with no red undertones.
- Ebony and black stains come out pewter.

Gray Wood is generally used with a graining tool.
- Gives black grain when used with a graining tool and dark stains
- Gives fresh new looks when grained over Bleached Wood with lighter colors
- Does not contain the red or brown undertones normally found in wood

What brand of stain works best on liquid wood?

Most wood stains work well on Retique It ® liquid wood. Some are much easier to use than others. I recommend Varathane Premium Fast Dry, Old Masters® wood stain, Sherwin Williams® wood stain, or any brand of gel stain. We have found that the Premium Fast Drying stains are the easiest to work with.

I do not recommend penetrating stains with Retique It ® liquid wood. Penetrating stains require a thicker wood surface to work properly. Retique It ®'s thin layer of wood does not allow enough penetration for these older-technology stains. Always follow the instructions on the can of the wood stain you choose. Absorption time varies by brand and product line.

What surfaces will Retique It ® liquid wood work on?

Retique It ® liquid wood can be applied to anything from furniture to steel doors, laminates, masonry, PVC, MDF, glass and more. All of these and more can be turned into beautiful stained products. Retique It ® liquid wood will not adhere to silicone, wax, or other petroleum-based products.

Do I need special tools to apply Retique It ® liquid wood?

No, Retique It ® liquid wood can be applied with a standard paintbrush, paint roller, or paint sprayer at 4-6 mm thick.

How is a wood grain achieved?

The grain achieved will vary with choice of brush and technique. As you apply the product with a brush, the brush strokes create a surface texture that will appear as wood grain when the stain is applied. If you use a sprayer, you will save time and still create a beautiful, solid-wood appearance.

Using a graining tool takes it to a whole new level if you want a pronounced raised grain. If you want a contemporary look, you will likely not want to use a graining tool.

MICHELE CORWIN

How do I prepare my surface for Retique It® liquid wood?

Preparation is important with this product, just as with any other paint or stain. Remove any loose paint, dirt, grease, or other undesirable content for best results. Patch any unwanted holes or grooves in your project with putty or non-shrinkable painter's caulk. This product will not adhere to silicone caulk.

How long does it take for Retique It® liquid wood to fully cure?

Each layer of Retique It® liquid wood should be fully dried and cured within two hours. Check your wood stain and sealant for absorption and drying times.

What type of sealant or poly should I use?

The sealant you should use depends on the durability your project requires. The general rule is to use the same type of sealant you would if you were protecting a wood finished piece.

Cabinets / Furniture / Walls: Retique It® Polyacrylic, or any polyurethane products.

Flooring / Counter tops / Table tops: I recommend Polytique It Extreme Protection Polyurethane (Non-Yellowing / Water-based) or another poly/sealant made for flooring. Fiddes Hard Wax Oil is made for flooring, and it gives fantastic protection, but keep in mind that it will yellow your white and gray surfaces.

Can I use Retique It® liquid wood for outdoor projects?

The interior version of Retique It® liquid wood does not provide protection against the UV rays of the sun. If you are using it for a project that will be in a shaded outdoor area, you can use a spar varnish to protect the finish. It will not hold up to direct sunlight longterm.

There is also an exterior version of Retique It® liquid wood. It dries in fifteen minutes, and can handle the UV rays of the sun. It works great for exterior projects when paired with an exterior stain and top coat. Unlike the interior version, It is not low-VOC, and it must be used outdoors or in a well ventilated area.

> **QUICK TIP**
>
> I recommend allowing your stain to dry for at least twenty-four hours prior to applying your top coat. The surface must not be tacky at all, or else an oil-based top coat like polyurethane will pull up your stain. Drying time depends a lot on humidity and how thickly you applied the stain.

Retique It liquid wood references a restorative product sold by Renaissance Innovations LLC which is a liquid product that contains 11% emulsified wood by weight, and is 66% wood by volume. Retique It®, the content in this book, and any trademarks referenced in this book are not associated with, nor is such content endorsed by, the trademark LIQUIDWOOD®, or its owner Abatron, Inc.

Retique It® is a registered trademark of Renaissance Innovations LLC

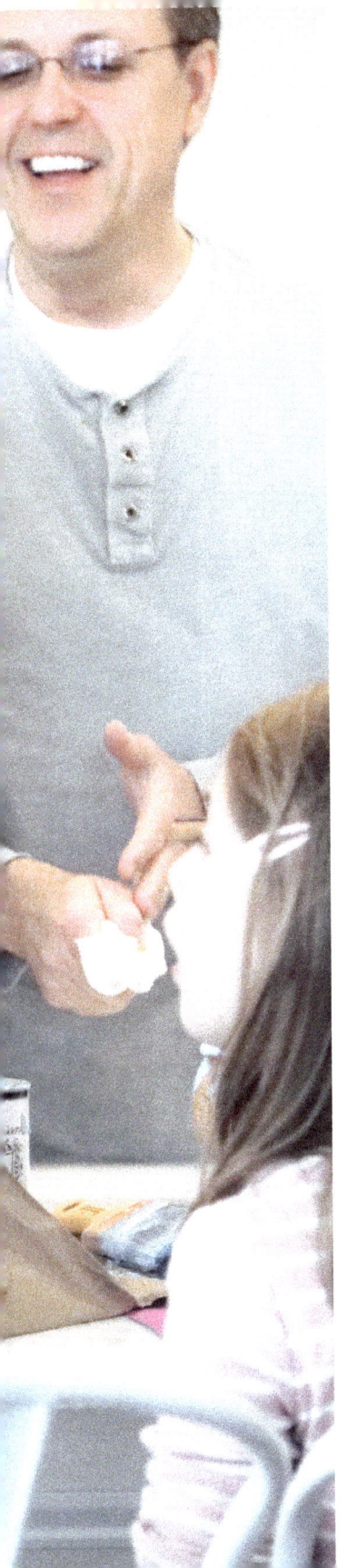

THANK YOU.

I truly don't have enough words to thank all the family and friends in my life who have encouraged me to share my journey through this book. I will attempt to name a few...

I would like to express my special gratitude to all my family who helped me get this book going. To Mom (Diane Lillard) and Dad (Michael Lillard), Grandma Stansbury (Delores Stansbury), Uncle Steve (Steven Lillard) and Aunt Marsha (Marsha Lillard), who took the time to guide and encourage me to finish this book.

Thanks to everyone on the Renaissance Innovations team who helped me so much. They tirelessly do the heavy lifting (literally) for all of us. A special thanks to Paola Amparan, whose keen eye and creative design helped make this book go beyond everything I had envisioned. I could not have done this without her and I'm forever grateful.

Thank you to my editors: Will Walton for his sense of humor and encouragement throughout the editing process, and Talia Smart for her attention to detail in bringing it all together.

Thank you to my children, who inspire me every day and put up with my daily talk of furniture and paint. May you never forget to let inspiration guide you in everything you do. And last but not least...thank you to my husband, James Corwin, who has always believed in me and my dreams, even when I had all but given up.

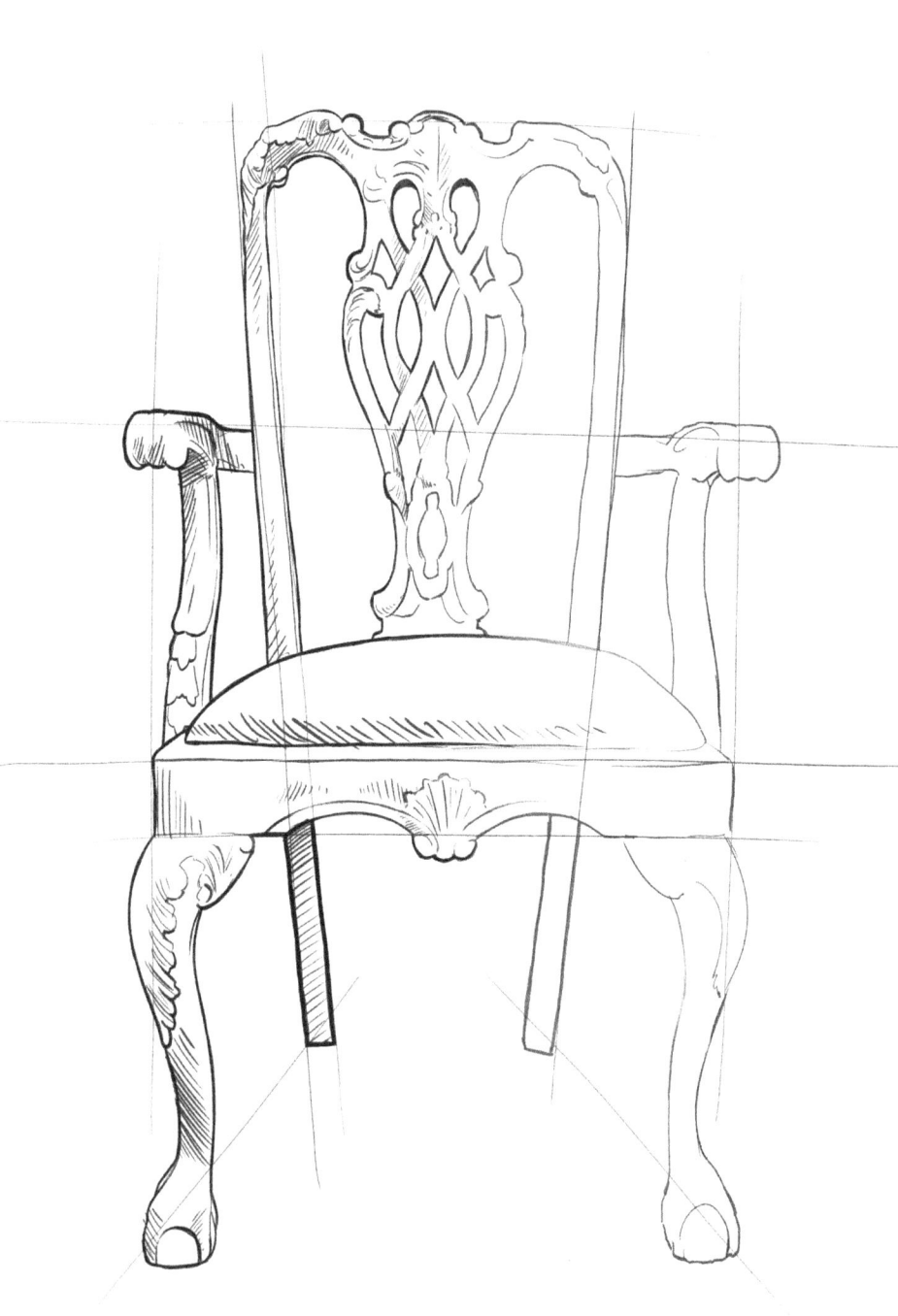

CPSIA information can be obtained
at www.ICGtesting.com
Printed in the USA
LVHW050532171219
640672LV00014B/761/P